Advance praise for
New Thinking New Politics

Your book was not written out of your own understanding but guided by the spirit of the living God … I am blessed by your insight, vision, mission and purpose defined and referenced in your amazing book - *New Thinking New Politics*.

Prof. Babs Onabanjo
President/CEO: A. D. King Foundation, Georgia, USA

Awesomely, awesome attempt you have here. In *New Thinking New Politics*, Samuel Adeyemi lays it bare like never before. His choice of words are simple, sincere and lucid. The best part of his attempt at expressing his thoughts is his emphasis on the emotional connection in politics. Coincidentally, emotional branding is the new frontier globally. Brands must adapt or Die.
I highly recommend this book for anyone and everyone interested in pushing the frontiers of relationship based exchanges.
This is a MUST have...
MUST read.

Charles O'Tudor
Global Brand INNOVENTOR
ADSTRAT BMC Limited

In this thought provoking bold faced exposé, Samuel Adeyemi expertly reveals that only an amalgam of powerful oratory, sound economic principles and a potent spiritual backbone can upgrade Africa from a poor house into a powerhouse.

The new era of African politics is fast becoming a cogent reality and proponents of this vision would find this book an invaluable read.

Johnson Abbaly
Founder, Agenda 2040

From musings on bloody revolutions to the failure of oratory, Adeyemi challenges the assumptions many Africans have made about their continent and their reality and insists - passionately - that they make new ones, and live through those values.

The message is urgent.

Chude Jideonwo
Managing Partner, RED

Samuel's book provokes introspection with his approach of combining secular leadership preparation nuggets with spiritual references on the need to raise a new generation of leaders for Nigeria, a nation whose potential has been severely undermined by underwhelming leadership. His emphasis on reworking the thought process founded on character and integrity within the Nigeria political space is also instructive.

For anyone interested in politics, dedicated to service and purpose for a better nation, this book is an excellent starter.

Oluseun Onigbinde
Co-Founder, BudgIT

Compelling and instructive, Samuel's book is indeed a curtain raiser for the new kind of politics that is about to hit Africa. It is a must-read if you're interested in positively impacting the politics of Africa.

Dr. David Kriz
Futurist/CEO, KrizDavid Foresight

New Thinking New Politics is a masterpiece of art that explores the current decadence in African political landscape and how the "new breeds" with right thinking and ideology can upstage the current trend. It cuts across various challenges these new breeds of African must take on before such an upstage can be a reality, including building right lines of thought, strong character and reputation, and strong spiritual prowess. The book also defines new political channel for aspiring new-breed politicians. I strongly recommend this book for all African youths and those who look forward to a new dawn in African polity.

Ayobami Ilori
Doctoral Candidate and Graduate Teaching Assistant, Department of Economics, University of Sheffield, United Kingdom

This is a really good book. ... I love the practical approach with lots of examples. Apart from giving readers a pattern it shows that you are widely read yourself... Overall it is a well-thought out book. Well done!

Philip Amiola
Co-founder, Panacea e-library

NEW
THINKING
NEW
POLITICS

Africa's transformation playbook for new breed politicians

Samuel O. Adeyemi

©2017 Samuel O. Adeyemi
www.samueladeyemi.com
samuel@samueladeyemi.com
@DemocratSam | +2348054259757

ISBN:978-978-962-744-8
Published in Nigeria by
Media DNA
20, Safaratu Sekoni Street, Gbagada, Lagos, Nigeria
books@mediadna.com.ng
+2348093061333

Cover Design by: *Solarspeaks +2348173933821*

Dedication

To everyone who thought and taught about the new Africa; may you be alive to enjoy the greatness of the continent when it is listed among the world powers.

TABLE OF CONTENTS

Dedication
Introduction
Preface

PART 1: NEW THINKING
CHAPTER 1   18

THE DYNAMICS OF NEW THINKING
Change Your Thinking   19
Of New Thinking & Bloody Revolutions   20
What Can Hinder You From Thinking Right?   21

CHAPTER 2   25
HOW TO THINK RIGHT
Books   25
Inspiring Speakers   31
Your Company   39
Goals and Visions   41
Your Goals in View   43
News for the Right Reasons   43

CHAPTER 3
THINK A NEW AFRICA   50
COMPONENTS OF NEW THINKING
Compassion   51
It Begets Vision   52
And Fuels Passion   53

Building Compassion — 54
Develop a Servant's Heart
Love People Genuinely — 55
The Power of Confidence — 56

CHAPTER 4
BUILDING SPIRITUAL MUSCLE — 59
More on Building Spiritual Muscle — 67
Start With A Small Battle — 71

CHAPTER 5
THE POWER OF REPUTATION — 77
Reputation Management — 78
Reputation in the Digital Age — 80
Your Online Reputation — 81
The Power of A Personal Profile — 84
Building A Strong Reputation — 85
Crisis Communication — 91

CHAPTER 6
THE POWER OF CHARACTER — 95
Reputation and Character — 97
How To Build Solid Character — 99
Accountability — 100
Mentorship — 101
Sincerity with Self
Help from God — 102

PART 2: NEW POLITICS
CHAPTER 7   **107**
THE HEART BIGGER THAN ANY POLITICAL PARTY
Of Political Parties
Of States of Origin & Ethnic Affiliations   *110*
The Scourge of Political godfatherism   *111*
Personal Transformation   *112*

CHAPTER 8   **116**
THE NEW POLITICIAN
The Power of Stagecraft
Political Intelligence   *118*
Campaign Intelligence
Retail Politics   *121*
Organise People
Entry Poll
Exit Polls   *122*

CHAPTER 9   **125**
THE POWER OF EMOTION
Emotional Home Truth   *131*

CHAPTER 10   **134**
ELECTION DAY
Your Field Agents
Leverage Technology   *135*
Ensure People go to the Polls
Your Victory and Concession Speeches   *136*
The God Factor

POST-ELECTION ACTIVITIES (IF YOU LOSE)

You're A Winner Anyway   *137*
Congratulating the Winner   *138*
Taking Stock
Constructive Criticism   *139*
Remaining Visible in A Strategic Way

POST-ELECTION ACTIVITIES (IF YOU WIN)

Thanking Voters   *140*
Preparing for Governance
Constituting Your Cabinet   *141*
Remaining Accountable to all Campaign Promises
Hitting the Ground Running   *142*
Keeping Your Guard Up

SIGN-OFF   **145**
Never Live Only for the History Books

BIBLIOGRAPHY   **146**

ACKNOWLEDGMENT   **152**

These men and women have come to fulfil prophecy.
There have never been a people like them and there will not be any
after them till the end of age.
The appearance of them is as the appearance of horses; and as
horsemen, so shall they run.
They will run like mighty men.
They will run on their path.
When they fall upon the sword, they shall not be wounded.[1]

INTRODUCTION

The idea for this book hit me in the middle of 2011. It came with a great sense of urgency to finish it up on time, lest I get enmeshed in another big project which will leave me with no time for the book. That was exactly what happened: The inspiration for the book came in torrents faster than my pen. In the midst of that, I got involved in a national political strategy and communication project that took close to five years of my life. I laboured day and night on the project. And, though it was an interesting project which broadened my horizon, I barely had time for myself – which invariably led to the near-abandonment of this book.

After agonising about it for about five months, I tendered my resignation and the rush of inspiration for the book came back immediately. Thus, within my one-month notice period, *New Thinking, New Politics,* was almost completed.

New Thinking, New Politics is a mixture of spiritual and intellectual reasoning! In your hand now is one of the most potent tools for winning any political battle in the new world order. In this political order, you do not have to play rough. All you need is to be well equipped to withstand any political force thrust at you.

This book is roundly soaked in spirituality; because the battle for the soul of Africa is spiritual. The battle will be won on the spiritual front before it manifests in the physical realm. All known methods have been deployed by numerous people to change Africa's fortune; unfortunately most have failed. Activism is good, but no amount of activism can change Africa's fortune.

Grammar is good; but no amount of oratory prowess can persuade those sitting on Africa's fortune to let go. Oration has no place in the spiritual. Sound economic principles are good; unfortunately, economic principles cannot make Africa a global economic powerhouse, in the absence of deep spiritual footing. It's high time we understood that there is need to combine activism, oratory prowess and sound economic principles with a strong spiritual muscle. That's the only way Africa can be rescued from this present state of hopelessness.

So, to change Africa, we have to think like our lives depend on thinking. To change Africa, we have to work like our lives depend on working. And above all, to change Africa, we have to engage spiritual mysteries like our lives depend on supernatural mysteries.

In this book, you will get hold of the secrets that will shape the new politics of Africa and ultimately, of the world. It is long overdue. The message has been passed across ages; from generation to generation. Now is the opportune time for this generation to witness it.

You will do well to combine the insights in this book with the revelation in *Righteous Man in Power* authored by my mentor, Bar. Kayode Adeniji. The book is a classical guide on war, leadership, and political strategy for sincere people, desiring change in the present dangerous political scene of Africa.

I hereby congratulate you because you now have in your hands the tools for winning in the new political realities of Africa!

PREFACE

It's time to change our thinking. Politics as we know it in Africa is about to take a new shape. Africa and the world is about to witness the arrival of a new breed of politicians. Theirs is an anointed politics that will challenge the status-quo. Of wisdom and brilliance, they are. They are strong spiritually, intellectually, and emotionally. In far-flung corners of the earth, they dwell.

Shoulder to shoulder, they make towards the goal. Their bond is as thick as rock. There is no breaking their rank. Though far too long, politics, especially in Africa is synonymous with greed, inept ideas, grand scale corruption and political assassination; however, there is a new generation bursting loose! They are equipped with the right tools to mend the broken down walls of the polity. People are much pained in their eyes. Behind them is a desolate land.

Ahead of them is a green pasture the world has never seen. They are determined. They are creative. They are formidable. They scale every hurdle. Not curtain by time and space, they soar on eagles wings. And, when they fall on the sword; they will not be wounded!

In them is the answer that will make Africa a world power!

PART 1

NEW

THINKING

There is a place the fierce eyes of the vultures have not seen.
There is a path no bird knows.[2]

NEW
THINKING

CHAPTER 1

THE DYNAMICS OF NEW THINKING

Taking giant leaps into the realm of possibilities demands a drastic change in thinking. The fact that you have not seen the new Africa does not mean it is not a reality. Africa may look broken and left behind now; but the time for Africa to be a world power is here.

The next big thing that will happen on Africa's political scene will be ushered in by the new thoughts enunciated in this book. Africa has stayed too long on this mountain. The continent has stayed too long on the mountain of despair, ridicule, poverty, lack, etc. It's time to leave behind this mountain which is a desolate land; because ahead of us is the Garden of Eden. In our lifetime, African countries will be listed among the world powers. African nations will flourish politically and economically.

The world will come to know God in Africa. Africa will export huge army of aid workers across the world. Africa will feed the world. No longer will there be visionless leaders at the helm of affairs in Africa.

The travel passports of African nations will become ultra valuable. Many so called strong nations in the world now will push and shove to get into Africa. No brigandage. No rigging of elections. No manipulation. Elections across Africa are about to be free and fair. The godfathers manipulating things across the length and breadth of the continent of Africa are about to be sent out of business and rendered jobless. Why? They will have no more value to offer.

Change Your Thinking

It is an established fact that the pattern of thinking of every human being dictates the direction of his or her life. From the Holy Book, we are made to understand that there is a direct relationship between the dominant thought patterns of a group, community or nation and the direction in which their pendulum of change will swing.

In the course of growing up and in my professional career as a journalist, political and media consultant, I have seen and participated in politics up-close – from the grassroots and on to the national stage as a volunteer and consultant. This rich experience has given me rare insights into how the mind of the average African voter, and the informed African politician trying to clinch his vote, functions.

> *In our lifetime, African countries will be listed among the world powers. African nations will flourish politically and economically.*

From political assassinations to corruption, intimidation, harassment, molestation, occultism; there is no limit to what some politicians in Africa will delve into, in order to win elections. In order to fortify themselves and have some advantage over their opponents, many have sold their souls to the kingdom of darkness. They have covenanted their lives, that of their families, the country and the continent to the dark forces which are holding Africa in perpetual bondage.

Hitherto, we have known all these vices as peculiar to Africa. However, I have news for you: all those vices are about to end. To make indelible transformation in politics, you don't have to sell your soul. I say this because in the coming dispensation, it is only those with a heart of service to the people who will have access into the palace.

Of New Thinking & Bloody Revolutions
Most people have resigned to fate, believing that Africa is doomed. They believe that the continent has come to the point of no return. Some who have faint hope believe that Africa's solution is embedded in a bloody revolution.

Listen! The only true and lasting revolution that will change Africa for good is the mind-set revolution. A revolution of the mind across Africa will catapult the continent into the league of world powers. Never again will Africa be taken for granted. The solutions to the myriad of challenges bedevilling Africa are simple. It won't take complex answers. It only needs a change in perspective and thinking. It demands a new paradigm shift. It takes seeing the unseen. It takes valuing the intangible over the tangible.

What Can Hinder You From Thinking Right?

Culture! Culture! Culture! That's the biggest enemy this continent is facing and must conquer. Culture shapes thinking. Culture shapes perspective. Culture has influenced Africa beyond what any policies or politics have ever done in a lifetime. Africa's culture can be felt in every sphere, including the political scene! Culture and tradition have determined how we elect our leaders; culture and tradition have made us tolerate inept political leadership through the years.

A wise man once said that culture and tradition can eat revelation for lunch. Indeed, no matter how fired up you are to see the potentials in Africa to become a world power, once you allow yourself to be entrapped in the

> *No matter how you do it, if you're bonded to the tradition and culture of Africa, you won't think of the new Africa.*

culture and traditions of Africa, you are sure to relapse and begin to talk like a mere being – when you are supposed to be a god!

Some parts of the African culture have held down millions of people from recognising and maximising their potentials. Come to think of it, do you realise that many so-called traditions and the culture we hold dear across Africa are nothing but modernized bondage? Do you know that many (not all) "wise sayings" that have been passed from generations to generations are actually full of ignorance?

Which culture do we hold dear? A culture of waste, where spending is made excessively on what's not needed. For example, you see someone who got a windfall and instead of investing that money in a venture that would employ people, he would rather throw a party and paint the town red, marrying new wives and 'terrorising' his neighbours with *I better pass my neighbour*[3] gadgets and wonders on wheels. So many traditions of Africa neither value nor cherish the intangibles. Creativity is not cherished in this kind of culture. Creativity is stifled.

No matter how you do it, if you're bonded to the tradition and culture of Africa, you won't think of the new Africa. Before you attempt to turn your back on the retrogressive culture and traditions the African continent hold dear, have this in mind: Anyone who comes against the culture of Africa will lead in the coming dispensation but not without strong opposition.

However, I can assure you that despite the fierce opposition, you're coming out victorious and will lead Africa into her golden era - the era which no mere mortal can comprehend or understand.

THINK!

• *In our lifetime, African countries will be listed among the world powers.*

• *African nations will flourish politically and economically.*

• *Listen! The only true and lasting revolution that will change Africa for good is the mind-set revolution. A revolution of the mind across Africa will catapult the continent into the league of world powers.*

• *No matter how you do it, if you're bonded to the tradition and culture of Africa, you won't think of the new Africa.*

HOW TO THINK
RIGHT

CHAPTER 2

HOW TO THINK RIGHT

Aligning your thinking the right way is not a stroll in the park. It is a battle. It is a fight. It is hard work. When you think right, your life will be right, your family will be right, your community will be right and your world will be right. Thoughts control your emotions, carriage and the words you speak.

Many may not realise it, but an average African's thoughts are shaped by culture and tradition. And that has pushed Africa into the claws of poverty and backwardness. One of the potent weapons we will use to create the Africa of our dream is to think right and see possibilities in our continent. Our challenge is not our colour but our character. It is not racism but the manner in which we relate with one another.

So, how do you program yourself to think right?

Read Books
Yes, you read that well. READ BOOKS. Not just books, but great books. Read books that edify and inspire. Read the Scriptures to see possibilities. When you read good books, you see what others are not seeing and you are empowered to do what others

are not doing.

Books have a huge capacity to alter the way you think about issues. A truly bookish fellow is not tied down by the parochial arguments of the political rightists or leftists, as s/he weighs and judges issues based on their own merit.

Those who don't read are servants of those who read. That's why Africa has been going cap in hand around the world looking for aids, instead of adding real value to the rest of the world. That's why Africa's resources have been taken out of the continent at a ridiculously cheap price and brought back at an extravagant price.

Those who will lead Africa into the 4th Industrial Revolution and the Promised Land must carry the "spirit of books."

Read across your field of expertise. Read beyond your age. Read between the lines. Read outside of the lines. When you're a voracious reader, you will know something about everything.

Read for pleasure. Read for entertainment. Read to be informed. Read to be reformed. Read to reset your mentality. Read classics. Read

One of the potent weapons we will use to create the Africa of our dream is to think right and see possibilities in our continent.

contemporary books. Read spiritual books. Don't be limited; read wide.

Yes, it's very important to be a voracious reader by reading everything in print and online, but in the course of reading, know what you're reading. Don't stuff your mind with junk. If you read junk; you act out junk. Garbage in, garbage out, remember?

I can testify to the power of books. Over the years, books have shaped my life. Reading has made me a better person. Through books, I have been able to commune with the immortals of ages.

I value books. At an early age, I made it a point of duty to ensure that the value of my books is more than that of my wardrobe.

> *Read across your field of expertise. Read beyond your age. Read between the lines. Read outside of the lines. When you're a voracious reader, you will know something about everything.*

Whenever I have a windfall, there's a place I have to restrain myself from visiting: the bookshop. However, like a magnet to metal filings, I can't resist its beckoning. My entrance into a bookshop often results in an empty wallet. Worse still, if there is a Point of Sales (POS) machine, my green account may well turn red!

Few years ago - shortly before gaining admission into the College of Journalism - while working for a retail company at Computer Village, Ikeja, Lagos, I remember going into a bookshop to get stationery for our company. On entering the bookshop, Bill Clinton's newly released autobiography, *My Life*, sat majestically on the shelf, winking earnestly at me. The book beckoned. Its aroma anaesthetized me.

"How much?" I managed to utter those two words to the shop attendant. "N5, 000!" He replied.

How can I raise this amount? I asked rhetorically. Standing there, I had only the N200 given to me from the office to buy stationery and my brand new Nokia 1100.

After much haggling over the price of the book, the shop attendant decided to slash a paltry N300 from the price tag of the book, and I promised to come back for it after buying the stationery. Then I headed back to the office.

At the office, the thought of the book wouldn't cease to dance in my head. I devised a plan to raise the money. The plan? Sell my cherished and brand new Nokia 1100 phone!
Oh, my Nokia 1100: then the fastest-selling phone at Computer Village, Ikeja, Lagos.

Oh my Nokia 1100: arguably, one of the most-stylish phones in the market then, with its stunningly big keypads.
Oh my Nokia 1100 – one of the first Nokia phones to come with FM Radio.

Compared to my Nokia 1100, the thought of being part of the first set of people to commune with Bill Clinton in his memoir was irresistible and more compelling. Eventually, I let go of my Nokia 1100. I sold it! Few minutes after, I returned to the bookshop to get the book. I bought it!

Till date, it is one of the most cherished books in my library. Buying the book was worth it. As I write, Nokia 1100 is obsolete and not in the market anymore but the book remains valuable to me.

As you know, writers don't die. Books don't die. When you write a book, you become immortal. When you read good books, you enter into the realm of the immortal. And, as Rev. Sam Adeyemi, would always say: "The Word Works Wonders!" Books – good books – also work wonders.

As a new breed politician, you may constantly be living with the fear of death, spiritual attack and physical attack. In this regard, inspired book can come handy. I will recommend *Fulfilling Your Days... Scriptural Principles for Long Life* written by Dr. David Oyedepo.

After buying and devouring the above mentioned book, I came to the realization that I cannot die anyhow. That there are invisible and fiery angels on guard, taking charge of my life. I came to know that the decision to live or die was mine to make. By reading the book, I knew for sure that death has been swallowed up in victory. The book is highly recommended for you in case you're plague with the spirit of death!

You can't amount to much in this new era of politics if you are not a lover of books. It's those books that will shape your thinking and make you do the right thing.

If you desire to be the president of your nation, you must also desire to consume memoirs of past and present presidents/leaders of advanced nations around the world. Do you desire to be a political strategist? Be voracious in reading materials of political scientists and strategists around the world.

Apart from reading materials relating to politics, reading wide is non-negotiable; because as a politician and leader, you will be making decisions on issues like the economy, security, health, transportation, information technology, etc.

Again, that's the reason you have to read wide. A wise man once said that an educated person is he that knows something about everything. In reality, knowing something about everything can't stop you from specialising, it will only make you rounded. If you are desirous of thinking right and making Africa great, you need good books.

> *Do you desire to be a political strategist? Be voracious in reading materials of political scientists and strategists around the world.*

Reading energises you
By reading this book, I know for certain that a surge of spiritual strength is running through your soul while your physical body will experience a new level of strength.

Listen to Inspiring Speakers

Don't just listen to anybody, listen to inspiring speakers. What you hear continuously will eventually become part of your life because who you listen to continuously speaks to your life. There is a spirit tied to the words that people speak which eventually shapes your thinking.

Believe me, who you listen to will surely shape your way of life and thinking. When you listen to complainers, very soon you will be a chief complainer instead of taking action. When you listen to those that have dreams and solutions, you will be impregnated with solutions and ideas to change our world.

Take a look into history; great people always refer to those who inspired them. The non-violence stand of the iconic Dr. Martin Luther King Jnr. was inspired by Mahatma Ghandi. Dr. King said that Gandhi's philosophy is *"the guiding light of our technique of non-violent social change."*

In his first book, *Stride Towards Freedom,* Dr. King expatiates on how he got magnetised and baptised into Ghandi. He notes, in the chapter called "Pilgrimage to Nonviolence", that during his enrolment at Crozer Theological Seminary (1948-51), Dr. Mordecai Johnson, the President of Howard University, delivered an electrifying sermon at the Fellowship House of Philadelphia.

Before this sermon, Dr. Johnson had recently visited India. He spoke glowingly about Gandhi's nonviolent resistance against the colonial rule of the British.

He writes:

> *His message was so profound and electrifying that I left the meeting and bought a half dozen books on Gandhi's life and works.*

That was how Dr. King's Christian beliefs were mixed with that of Ghandi's nonviolent resistance which propelled him into the hearts of millions across the globe; and forever he is remembered in the history books.

Just as Dr. King was inspired by Ghandi; so was Bill Clinton inspired by Dr. King.

While writing about how much Martin Luther King Jnr's "I Have a Dream" speech inspired him in his bestselling autobiography, *My Life*, Bill Clinton states in chapter eight of the book:

> *One other memorable event happened to me in the summer of 1963. On August 28, nine days after I turned seventeen, I sat alone in a big white reclining chair in our den and watched the greatest speech of my lifetime, as Martin Luther King Jr. stood in front of the Lincoln Memorial and spoke of his dream for America. In rhythmic cadences reminiscent of old Negro spirituals,*

his voice at once booming and shaking, he told a vast throng before him, and millions like me transfixed before television sets, of his dream that "one day on the red hills of Georgia, the sons of former slaves and the sons of former slave owners will be able to sit down together at the table of brotherhood," and that "my four little children will one day live in a nation where they will not be judged by the colour of their skin but by the content of their character."

It is difficult to convey more than forty years later the emotion and hope with which King's speech filled me; or what it meant to a nation with no Civil Rights Act, no Voting Rights Act, no open housing law, no Thurgood Marshall on the Supreme Court; or what it meant in the American South, where schools were still mostly segregated, the poll lux was used to keep blacks from voting or to round them up to vote as a bloc for the status quo crowd, and the word "nigger" was still used openly by people who knew better.

I started crying during the speech and wept for a good while after Dr. King finished. He had said everything I believed, far better than I ever could. More than anything I ever experienced, except perhaps the power of my grandfather's example, that speech steeled my determination to do whatever I could for the rest of my life to make Martin Luther King Jr.'s dream come true.

Indeed, millions around the world are witnesses to the great works that Bill Clinton did within his ability to bring to pass the dream of Dr. King.

Dr. Nnamdi Azikiwe (Nigeria's first President after independence in 1960) was born into a relatively comfortable household and shielded from the pains and shackles that most Africans were subjected to under the colonial rule. His father was a top civil servant and was hoping that one day he will replace him in the Civil Service.

Dr. Azikiwe lived this normal life until the age of 16years when he listened to a sermon by Reverend Doctor James Emmanuel Kwegyir Aggrey at Tinubu Methodist Church, while a student and boarder at the Wesleyan Boys' High School. In his autobiography, *My Odyssey*, Dr. Azikiwe writes:

> *I listened to a sermon which saturated my whole being. I became spiritually electrified. It then dawned upon me that life had a meaning and I had a mission to fulfil; thus it was my task to make life worthwhile for my fellow men and to be a friend to struggling humanity.*

According to Dr. Azikiwe, the preacher "delivered an inspiring message" from Isaiah 6:1-10. He continues:

> *Soft and melodious, his voice struck my soul with the force of a supernatural wand. Symbolic and suave, his*

message found my heart
a ready soil for the dreams of a new social order.

Dr. Azikiwe affirms that the sermon was "magnetic" and the sentence that stuck with him forever is 'Nothing but the best is good for Africa'. "As he uttered these words, the scales fell from my eyes and I began to see a glorious future," so writes Dr. Azikiwe. He submits that "From that day, I became a new man, and my ideas of life changed so much that I lived in daydreams, hoping against hope for the time it would be possible for me to be like Dr. Aggrey."

Chief Obafemi Awolowo (the first premier of the Western Region of Nigeria) in Chapter 6 of his autobiography, *Awo,* writes about how the great Nigerian nationalist, Herbert Macaulay, enchanted and awakened his political consciousness:

> *The spell and the impact which the personality and the view of Herbert Macauly cast and made on me must have been enchanting and profound. We were regular and voracious readers of the Lagos Daily News, as well as conscientious believers in the opinions expressed in that paper. Back in 1922, my young mind had been saturated with the belief that the late Herbert Macauly was the champion and defender of Native Rights and Liberty.*
> *This belief must have been engendered by almanacs and calendars which carried Herbert Macauly's*

photographs together with eulogistic captions on the man's political exploits, and by adulatory remarks made to my hearing about him by elders.

Readers, these examples have showed the power of listening to great men and women. My dear readers, inspiration is powerful. I don't listen to just anybody; I listen to those who can ignite fire in my belly.

My world view has been shaped by inspiring speakers. The touch of inspired words from my mentors and spiritual parents has turned me into another man - determined to ensure that African nations are listed among the world powers.

> *When you're discouraged or bored, listening to your favourite inspirational speaker will go a long way to ginger you back to life.*

Some years ago, in a rundown classroom at St. Joseph Secondary School, Agege, Lagos, Nigeria; I was a high school student; Kayode Adeniji, (now an author of repute, thinker and lawyer) was a Law student at the Lagos State University (LASU).

As the founder of the Art Department Club (a club he founded while still in secondary school and at the age of 15), he came to inspire Art students who gathered together from different secondary schools in Agege. Not minding that our small brains   may not adequately capture the picture he waspainting,   he spoke passionately about the coming revolution that will hit the continent of Africa.

That speech, in a rundown classroom on that hot afternoon, set an unquenchable fire within me even till now. Like the cup-bearer in the scriptures, Bar. Adeniji is still carrying the same message of revolution and with greater depth and insight.

He has authored a great book, *Righteous Man in Power* - a book on Politics, War and Strategy for sincere people who have a calling in the dangerous political scenes of Africa. It is a survival guide and strategy for any sincere politician. If you have a calling in politics, it is a must read!

> *The road to Africa's real change may be long and torturous. Therefore, you need inspiration to stay on course. You need inspiration as a medication when you're becoming weary and tired.*

On yet another evening, we sat together in his mother's house somewhere in Agege, then a slum in Lagos, Nigeria. That night, he began expounding on the coming revolution that will hit Africa from the book of Joel in the Scriptures.
The revelation from that night has not left me. It continues to

intoxicate me.

When you're discouraged or bored, listening to your favourite inspirational speaker will go a long way to ginger you back to life. In the late 90s, while holidaying in one of my aunt's house, I felt a strong frustration about the situation in my country, Nigeria. At that particular moment, a soft voice boomed out of the radio in the room.

The voice was that of Sam Adeyemi, host and President of Success Power International. He spoke on why we should not give up on Nigeria and painted a picture of the great things that will come to this great nation.

There was another time I was listening to an old CD of his entitled 'Sophisticated Wisdom'. In the message, he prophesised about the new Nigeria. That message has inspired me not a few times and continues to do same up till this present moment.

> *In essence, surrounding yourself with those who will hold your hand and you accountable to your actions will ensure that your thinking is set on the right path.*

Those encounters are indelible. They keep me going, knowing that Nigeria will be great and that the glaring challenges in the country will be a thing of the past. The road to Africa's real change may be long and torturous. Therefore, you need inspiration to stay on course. You need inspiration as a medication when you're becoming weary and tired.

Inspiration is the engine that propels every change agent. Please note that there is a difference between motivation and inspiration. The former is momentary while the latter is eternal.

> *Having visions and goals that have people at its core enlarges your heart. It makes you think right. Your heart will constantly beat for the people.*

You can't be hit by inspiration and remain normal. Motivation is just to excite you for a while; while inspiration will stay with you for a long time. Therefore, be inspired!

Choose Your Company Carefully

The Holy Book said it all:

> *He that walks with wise men shall be wise: but a companion of fools shall be destroyed.*

There is no way you can be an active participant in the revolution that is coming to the continent of Africa if your close friends, mentors and closest advisers believe that Africa is destined to be backward until the end of age. When you befriend those that constantly jeer at your vision to change

Africa; very soon, you will lose steam and fizzle out of the race to change Africa.

Dr. David Oyedepo said, "They that walk, walk with many. They that run, run with a few. They that fly, fly alone." Who you decide to pitch your tent with will determine what portion of greatness awaits you. It is better to be friendless than to be in the midst of those that will drain you of emotional and spiritual energy.

> *Having goals and visions for the new Africa will make you do some things today. And, of course, in contrast, because of your visions and goals, there are lots of things you will shy away from doing today.*

The next battle for the soul of Africa will be won and lost on spiritual fronts. So, you need to gird your loins. Surround yourself with sound and spiritual people. It is pertinent that I sound a note of warning here: spirituality has nothing to do with a pious disposition. One can wear a pious look without being pure at heart. What I am advocating is sincerity and purity of heart.

Spirituality, like righteousness, is a way of life. It is beyond works. It is that state of heart that constantly longs and desires to please God in whatever is done. It is that state of heart that knows to swiftly ask for forgiveness when a mistake is made. It is that state where grace is not taken for granted. It is that state of heart when sin no longer has dominion over you; when you reign above it.

In essence, surrounding yourself with those who will hold your hand and you accountable to your actions will ensure that your thinking is set on the right path.

Have Goals and Visions

It is essential to have goals and visions that set fire in your belly. I mean goals and visions that will keep you awake in the night. Goals and visions that see the people of Africa not the way they presently are but the way they can be when things are done properly.

> *If you don't consume news for the right reasons, you will be spiritually malnourished and sooner will be famished.*

The heart of a man that has the goal of just surviving and eating three meals a day is different from the heart of the man that has a goal and vision to feed millions of hungry people.

Likewise, the man whose heart pants after buying the latest jeep to jump across the potholes ridden roads of Africa is different from the heart of the man that constantly thinks about how to provide good road networks across the continent and make life better for the people.

When you think about how to cloth the naked and not just about what to wear; your goals and visions are full of grandeur. They are noble. They transcend from generation to generation. Having visions and goals that have people at its core enlarges your heart. It makes you think right. Your heart will constantly beat for the people.

Guess what? No one ever has a genuine heart for the people and becomes stranded. It's not possible. How can you produce millionaires and billionaires yet still live in penury? Impossible! So, enlarge your heart. Think big. Think about how to uplift huge numbers of people from poverty, sickness and malnutrition.

Unlike any other continent of the world, Africa's landscape is virgin, waiting to be cultivated. It is rich, waiting to unload its riches. Presently, no other continent of the world presents the opportunity to add value across borders on a massive scale like Africa does.

Some have postulated that Africa is the last frontier, and I do agree. Therefore, have a goal to change Africa for good. Have a goal to plug into every sphere of Africa and make it world-class, sought-after. Africa may not have profited maximally in the previous Industrial Revolutions; however, do have in mind that the Artificial Intelligence-powered Fourth Industrial Revolution will flourish in Africa.

Having goals and visions for the new Africa will make you do some things today. And, of course, in contrast, because of your visions and goals, there are lots of things you will shy away from doing today.

What do I mean? Because you have a glimpse into the future and see what is about to be unfolded, you will prepare today, you will act today, and you will put your dreams and visions to work today.

On the other hand, there are lots of things you will run away from doing today. You will not be involved in things that will tarnish your image in the future.

Keep Your Goals Close
In the journey to create a new Africa, bumpy roads are ahead that will discourage and may demoralise you. The way to stay inspired is to have your dreams and visions close which will serve as nourishment for your soul in times of challenge and discouragement. Keeping your goals and visions close will give you creative ideas on how to speedily achieve them.

Consume News for the Right Reasons
News by its very nature is bad news. We're told in Journalism school that when a dog bites a man, it's no news; but when a man bites a dog, then the network news of the world would be on a frenzy, running over one another to be the first to break the

breaking news!

The media regards good news as PR! The major news outlets of the world have built their business model on popularizing bad news. Bad news brings viewership to TV news. Bad news brings listeners to Radio. Bad news brings readers to newspapers both online and offline. It follows that more viewership, listeners, and readers mean advertising revenue which sustains the media industry across the world.

Without advertising revenue, media houses will be "dead on arrival." That is one of the reasons bad news crowds out good news in the world media. So, when you constantly consume news, your soul may be depressed and soaked in pessimism on the prospect for Africa.

I know what it means to be saturated with news. I understand what it means to start your day with the news. As a media consultant, political strategist and journalist, I consume an average of fifteen newspapers and news blogs daily.

I know what "cache" is dropped in my spirit after reading about civil wars, famine, poverty and corruption in Africa. That is why one needs to be careful about how much news is consumed on a daily basis.

If you don't consume news for the right reasons, you will be spiritually malnourished and sooner will be famished.

Consuming news indiscriminately will puncture your faith. You will become normal. You will complain like everybody. You will speak like everybody. You will think like everybody when you're supposed to be charting the course beyond the realities of your days.

Information is power. Information will power the revolution that will hit Africa. Go after information in the media but be sure to sieve what drops into your spirit.

THINK!

• One of the potent weapons we will use to create the Africa of our dream is to think right and see possibilities in our continent.

• Read across your field of expertise. Read beyond your age. Read between the lines. Read outside of the lines.

• Books – good books – also work wonders.

• Do you desire to be a political strategist? Be voracious in reading materials of political scientists and strategists around the world.

• If you are desirous of thinking right and making Africa great, you need good books.

THINK!

- When you're discouraged or bored, listening to your favourite inspirational speaker will go a long way to ginger you back to life.

- The road to Africa's real change may be long and torturous. Therefore, you need inspiration to stay on course.

- Surrounding yourself with those who will hold your hand and you accountable to your actions will ensure that your thinking is set on the right path.

- Having visions and goals that have people at its core enlarges your heart. It makes you think right. Your heart will constantly beat for the people.

THINK!

•Having goals and visions for the new Africa will
make you do some things today. And, of course,
in contrast, because of your visions
and goals, there are lots of things you will
shy away from doing today.

•If you don't consume news for the right
reasons, you will be spiritually malnourished
and sooner will be famished.

THINK A NEW
AFRICA

CHAPTER 3

THINK A NEW AFRICA

Life started in Africa. Life is coming back to Africa. I have been to the mountain top; I can see a great and prosperous Africa. I can see the Africa flowing with milk and honey. I can see African countries united and sending aids to the rest of the world.

I can see an Africa sold out to the agenda of God this end time. I can see an army of young and old people across Africa sold out to righteousness and walking in purpose, taking territories for God.

I have seen the Promised Land.
We will get there.
You, my reader, will get there.
I, the author, will get there.

COMPONENTS OF NEW THINKING

Dear reader, when you're sold out to the new Africa and your thinking is changed; there are some thought patterns that will propel your actions in your family, community and country.

This thought patterns will birth in you compassion, confidence, courage and strong character.

Compassion

Genuine compassion for people makes you create change. Compassion sets a fire burning inside you. You are much pained by sub-optimal living as observed around you. Nothing short of upstaging the status-quo will suffice. Compassion for the people you intend to serve will propel you to scale any hurdle set before you.

I can see an Africa sold out to the agenda of God this end time. I can see an army of young and old people across Africa sold out to righteousness and walking in purpose, taking territories for God.

For you to be successful in this dispensation of New Thinking New Politics, governance and politics will be seen and taken as a divine calling to serve God and humanity. This new era, passion will be the propelling force for people in governance. But to successfully complete this transition and change, passion is not enough; there is need for genuine compassion for people that speaks with every action.

To be compassionate, you must see people not the way they are but the way they should be. This will ignite an unquenchable inferno in your belly. Your steps will have springs! These springs will take you higher and higher into the heart of the people.

Compassion causes you to have a sense of urgency. It causes you to have an unending flow of creative thoughts. That creative juice that is extracted from you when you are compassionate is worth trillions and zillions in the best currency of the world! An idea that employs millions of people will be birthed when you are compassionate.

No one will ever serve successfully and lead in this new chapter of Africa's existence without genuine compassion for people.

> *No one will ever serve successfully and lead in this new chapter of Africa's existence without genuine compassion for people.*

Compassion Begets Vision

Earth-shaking visions are contacted on the path of compassion. The easiest path to having a vision that will propel the course of your life is simply to have compassion on the people you have been sent to. The path of compassion is a road less travelled in the old Africa's political system. No wonder, the politicians that held sway in this system are short-sighted, myopic and unable to see beyond their noses.

The ONLY reason you can succeed in the new Africa is that you have compassion on people. Have this in mind and inscribe it in your heart and soul: No Compassion; No Success. Grand visions are birthed on the altar of compassion. Our Lord Jesus Christ was able to perform all those miracles we read and marvel at in scriptures because He had compassion on the people of His time.

It will break His heart to see the newly wed disgraced on their wedding day, so He turned water to wine through compassion. It broke His heart to see families lose their loved ones; so He raised the dead through compassion. It broke His heart to see the crowds starving in the wilderness; so He fed them miraculously through compassion.

It broke his heart to see people living in lack and poverty; so He extracted money from fishes.

It broke his heart to see humanity lost and eternally separated from the Father; so he laid down his life. Compassion will make you do great and mighty things beyond what Jesus did while on earth. Compassion will make you have the vision to clothe the naked; house the homeless and feed the hungry. No nation and continent will ever be great except its leaders are visionaries. And this vision is a product of compassion. When you are compassionate; grand visions are assured.

Compassion Fuels Passion

Without compassion, your passion amounts to nothing and will fizzle out in no time! It is genuine compassion on people that fuels passion. In times of discouragement when pursuing your passionate cause, it is compassion that will hold you to stay the course. It is compassion that will make you stay on the message of a new Africa, even when everything around you is saying otherwise. It is compassion that will fuel your resolve to crush every corrupt element feasting on Africa's destiny.

Without compassion, you will discover that your message will be bland and very soon blown away by every "wind of doctrine." Being genuinely compassionate on the people of Africa will ensure that your passion will always be strong.

BUILDING COMPASSION

Compassion like every other trait of a leader can be learnt and imbibed. How do you then build compassion into your life in order to be part of the army of real and genuine change agents rising up across Africa?

Develop a servant heart

A servant is always at the beck and call of his master. When Robert Greenleaf developed the concept of 'Servant Leadership'[6] in an essay he first published in 1970, he argued that Servant Leadership begins with the natural feelings that one wants to serve first.

> *A servant leader's allegiance is first to serve God, and then to serve humanity. Not even your political affiliation should derail that mandate.*

That conscious choice brings one to aspire to lead. The Servant Leader ensures that other people's highest priority needs are served and met. Similarly, having a servant heart makes you to be conscious of your divine mandate to serve, irrespective of the personal inconvenience that may arise in the process.

54

A servant leader's allegiance is first to serve God, and then to serve humanity. Not even your political affiliation should derail that mandate. The good news is that servant leadership is not the exclusive preserve of a few. Everyone can do it. Everyone can serve. Therefore, everyone can lead. That is why this new generation of Africans that subscribe to change their thinking will redefine politics and leadership in Africa.

Servant leadership will make you roll up your sleeves and get into the trenches to ensure that things are done the right way. Servant leadership will ensure that you trade your personal convenience for your people's convenience. It is that state of heart that knows that no one should be left behind in the slope of growth and development in the social and economic lives of the continent. Servant leadership is the key if you must have and demonstrate genuine compassion for the people of Africa.

Love People Genuinely

Love makes you to surmount any obstacle to be of service to people. Love covers a multitude of sins. Loving people wholeheartedly ensures that you pour all your being into their service. When people talk, you listen. You're not preoccupied

> *Confidence charges you towards the opposition and makes for an easy triumph.*

with your ideas and not necessarily forcing your own ideas on them. You wear their shoes to know where it pinches.

Without love, compassion will not spring forth in you. It takes genuine love for the well-being of Africans for you to show compassion for them.

A note of warning here: don't allow the love of people to make you transgress against God. If it means standing alone, stand alone in your belief and resolve to please your creator first and foremost. Remember your first allegiance is to God, not people. People may derail you; God won't. The good news is that when you love God, you will love people as well by directing them aright.

The Power of Confidence
In this new era of New Thinking and Politics, we are up against deeply entrenched interests, principalities and powers. Those that have built corrupt political empires will not let go easily. The old orders will be ever so determined to stay the course. To disarm and subdue these forces, there is need for an unstoppable confidence to be embedded in you. Your confidence is a sure certificate of triumph in any battle. Without it, victory is not certain. That is why when the stage is set for confrontation, these forces against Africa reach for your confidence.

Confidence makes you dare the impossible! Confidence charges you towards the opposition and makes for an easy triumph. Oh, how we need confidence to actualise the dream of a great and prosperous Africa.   How do you build your confidence? This will be treated in the next chapter.

THINK!

•No one will ever serve successfully and lead in this new chapter of Africa's existence without genuine compassion for people.

•It is compassion that will fuel your resolve to crush every corrupt element feasting on Africa's destiny.

•A servant leader's allegiance is first to serve God, and then to serve humanity. Not even your political affiliation should derail that mandate.

•People may derail you; God won't.

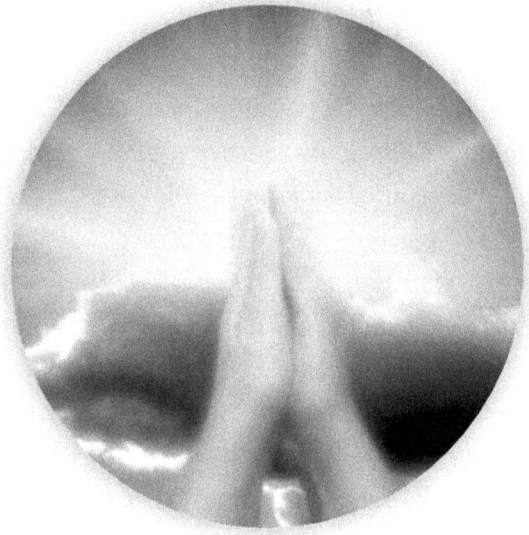

BUILDING SPIRITUAL
MUSCLE

CHAPTER 4

BUILDING SPIRITUAL MUSCLE

There is a strong link between spirituality and confidence. Confronting the challenges of Africa with our mental capabilities will amount to nothing. Building your spiritual muscle will entail 'eating' God's word and believing Him in every area of your journey in life. To build your spiritual muscle in order to have confidence, all you need is to lay hold on the promises of protection, provision and sure victory, as they are unfolded to you on the pages of scriptures and from anointed vessels.

The good news is that once you are sold-out to ignite change in your country and continent in line with God's agenda, you are supernaturally covered. You become untouchable, unmolestable, unmovable. You're like a rock – if you're attacked, the attacker breaks to pieces; and if you're on the offensive, the target is broken to pieces. To invoke this protection mentioned, commune regularly with the Almighty and gym constantly in the immortal and infallible words of God. Change makers must be deep spiritually, building their spiritual muscle by communing with the supernatural beyond this physical realm.

The battle between David and Goliath was won and lost on the spiritual front. David spoke. Goliath spoke. What made the difference is the power behind the words both spoke. David invoked the power of the Almighty God; Goliath cursed David in the name of his gods. Oration without deep spirituality is nothing but nursery rhymes. Nothing ever moves in this world except somebody moves it from the spiritual realm.

In this world, movers of things are in the minority. The Pareto's 80/20 principle comes to mind here. A cursory look at every stage of human civilization shows that people propelled by a spirit – either positive or negative – change the course of history. Change makers do not suddenly appear, lest they suddenly disappear! Jesus was underground, preparing for a great ministry by frequenting the temple to sit at the feet of the Rabbi and was later led into the wilderness to be tutored by the spirit.

> *Change makers must be deep spiritually, building their spiritual muscle by communing with the supernatural beyond this physical realm.*

In those periods, Jesus was building his spiritual muscle for the task ahead. And he did change the course of history. Consider the "preparation" of Barak Obama at the backside of Chicago where he was organising and touching peoples' lives away from the eyes of the national media.

It was in this period he came to know and accept Jesus Christ as his personal Lord and Saviour. "It was through that experience (community organising in Chicago) working with Pastors and lay people, trying to heal the wounds of hurting neighbourhoods that I came to know Jesus Christ myself and embrace him as my Lord and Saviour," Obama revealed at a National Prayer Breakfast in 2011.

> *Oration without deep spirituality is nothing but nursery rhymes.*

Spiritually is real. Spirituality is a leverage in politics. God is interested in the governing and the affairs of men and women on earth. The Psalmist says that the earth is the Lord's, and all its fullness. The Lord is spiritual; it follows therefore, that if you will dominate and reign on earth, you must be spiritual.

Dr. King is someone who left an indelible mark in history. Every speech of Dr. King Jnr. drips of spirituality. He never spoke a word like an orator. He spoke like an oracle. *"I Have a Dream"* and *"I Have Been to the Mountain Top"* are speeches soaked in spirit. These speeches are prophetic.

His words in these speeches have come and are still coming to pass. To drive home my point, let me paint a picture for you: The excitement in the main bowl was palpable, reaching feverish pitch. Shouts of joy welling out of the thousands parked into the arena were deafening.

Blue balloons and ribbons ascend and descend in a scenic beauty over the crowd. With millions watching on primetime belt and logged-on to the internet worldwide, that day was long-time coming. Surely, it was a historical moment! Notably, the day marked the 45th year that the preacher named Martin Luther King Jr, shared the dream he had. This was the fulfilment of prophecy.

The day? 2008 Democrats National Convention held in the state of Denver of United States to nominate Senator Barak Obama as the party's flag bearer in the coming election. This new bride of the Democrats just must deliver. The polls are not really favourable. He trails two points behind the Republican hopeful in the polls. The speech will either make or mar his chances. Superb performance was not negotiable, lest he slides further in the polls.

"Ladies and Gentlemen, the next President of …" the compère called. Backstage, the man of the moment stood, oblivious to the deafening noise in the arena; crossed his mouth with a finger, closed his eyes, said a short prayer and busted on stage; waving and acknowledging cheers. Millions of people watching all over the world and those shouting themselves hoarse in the main bowl missed this part where he communed with the immortal. What they saw was a presidential candidate full of energy, smiling and waving on stage.

In an electrifying voice, Senator Obama gave the speech of his life, winning over numerous independents and undecided voters. This instance was indeed the fulfilment of the prophecies of Dr. King. His oratory translated into something tangible.

As positive change igniters, you need to be sensitive to the Holy Spirit. When you hear from heaven, the actors on the political scene will have no choice but to listen to you. These actors may put up resistance; but know that it's cosmetic.

> *When your spiritual muscle is fully grown, you speak deep wisdom.*

The resistance won't stand the test of time. When you're in tune with the spiritual, your words will be potent, sharper than every two-edged sword! When your spiritual muscle is fully grown, you speak deep wisdom. Wisdom has no respect for age, race, and gender. Deep wisdom helps you to stand erect amid the firing arrows of your enemies. The scripture made it explicit – *wisdom is the principal thing.*

In preparing to cause change on the political scene, you need to be a man of the word. The world we live in is controlled by the word. The fallen principalities take charge of Africa's politics based on the weak words they possess and they will not let go easily. With the real words, they cannot but submit! Want to be in politics? You must be a wordsmith! Words sway emotions.

Words heal. Through the word, the world was made.

Fiery rhetoric has set the world on fire in times past. Hitler's rhetoric caused World War II; Winston Churchill's rhetoric soared Britain on the wings of victory during the war.

Good news – the word is God! God is the word! Get the word and you will control the world. Want to be a political orator? You need to gym continually in the word by reading the word of God. Sounds silly? Consider reading through the speeches of Dr. Martin Luther King Jnr. You'll see the words of God flashing out of every page. Still not convinced? Wait for this:

Perhaps you do not know that Senator Barak Obama climbed to national prominence based on one powerful speech that I discovered has its root in the scriptures. In 2004, as a nominee from the state of Illinois for the US Senate, Barak Obama was nominated by Senator John Kerry to give the keynote address at the convention.

The speech turned the crowd into an ecstasy. The press came out with a screaming headline the following day, proclaiming that a star had been born. The meat of that speech has its roots in Galatians 3:28. Grab your Bible and open that passage. Google up Obama's speech at the 2004 Democratic convention, compare the two and see what I am talking about:

There is neither Jew nor Greek, there is neither slave nor free, there is neither male nor female; for you are all one in Christ Jesus. **Galatians 3:28 (NKJV).**

... There is not a liberal America and a conservative America – there is the United States of America. There is not a Black America and a White America and Latino America and Asian American – there's the United States of America
-Barak Obama.

Can you glean the similarities between the Bible passage and the then US Senate candidate's speech? Do you know that John Maxwell mines 80% of the materials for his bestselling leadership books from the Bible? Though he seldom explicitly quotes the scriptures in his books, they are rooted in scriptures. When positive change makers hear from heaven, supernatural confidence is released to confront any known or unknown obstacle and usher in new politics.

Those that will change their thinking and align with the superior spirit that controls heaven and earth will subdue old order actors on Africa's political scenes. Their words will be potent, striking deep, sharper than any two-edge sword!

> *When positive change makers hear from heaven, supernatural confidence is released to confront any known or unknown obstacle and usher in new politics.*

When your spiritual muscle is fully grown, you speak with unquenchable confidence that drips with lots of wits and wisdom. Friends, this wisdom has no respect for gender, age, race or size! Supernatural wisdom is the principal thing. Deep wisdom cements your confidence to stand upright amid the fiery arrows of the enemies. That wisdom will propel your confidence to string words as a weapon to do battle. You need to be a man of the word! The world we live in is controlled by the word. The principalities holding hostage Africa's political scene and destiny have taken charge for too long based on the weak and counterfeit words they possess.

> *I can't guarantee that your spiritual leaders and mentors, by their actions and deeds, won't "embarrass" your political campaign.*

It was said of a certain man that when he spoke people clapped, but when another spoke people marched! What it means is that the former was an orator while the latter an Oracle.

Oratory will be useless in this new political era. Only oracles will have a say and way into peoples' hearts.

Our world needs oracles, not orators.
If you are reading this, and you have genuine love for your people, you have compassion, you have a solid character and competence, in this new era when you open your mouth to speak, people will march to cause positive change.

More on Building Spiritual Muscle

The issue of building your spiritual muscle cannot be over flogged. You are up against those that have covenanted their lives and that of a whole continent to the devil. Building your spiritual muscle requires that you have a more potent force. Politics is a full contact sport played on murky

When your spiritual muscle is fully grown, you speak with unquenchable confidence that drips with lots of wits and wisdom.

waters. Major players in this game belong to a secret society. To come out victorious, you need solid fortifications beyond your adversaries' secret societies. Many politician run from pillar to post for fortification. Human blood and other horrible things are used for sacrifices.

As an agent of positive change, you do not need all that. What you need is a superior 'secret society' that will swallow up every other secret society. Remember, *he that dwells in the secret place of the most high shall abide under the shadow of the almighty.*

So, if anyone asked you to come join any secret society for the sake of protection, fortification, power and building confidence, tell them you belong to a superior society that swallows up all other devilish secret societies claiming to be deciding the world's order.

As Moses' rod swallowed up every other rod of the magicians of Egypt, so also God's agenda for this generation is to swallow up any challenge standing against the people of destiny. Those that dwell in the secret place of the almighty are enveloped in mysteries and deep secrets, it takes a redeemed mind to assess it.

Those spiritually connected to this mystery are above every power and principality in this world. They are gods! They drink mystery blood and flesh (Communion).

This is the real body and blood of the living God; whereas, members of the kingdom of darkness, at most, drink the blood of human beings and that of chickens. Which is superior? The blood of chickens, humans or Jesus Christ's? That of the Living God, of course! This is the foundation of our confidence in the battle for the soul of Africa. Your thinking will change when you understand this mystery. You are more than a conqueror! Your confidence and victory are sealed and stamped! When you belong to God, you are like a wind. The world cannot figure you out. They can't understand! You're presented with an infallible political playbook which will dazzle your opponents and adversaries every single time.

Of Spiritual Leaders

Writing in his bestselling book, *The Audacity of Hope,* Senator Obama narrated how he encountered God in the church and how his pastor greatly influenced his life. The title of that book was taken from one of the messages of his pastor, Rev. Jeremiah

Wright. Though his pastor committed some gaffes during his presidential campaign that nearly capsized his political fortune, he still kept faith in his pastor.

In a speech entitled 'For a More Perfect Union' given to assuage the concerns of his supporters, he kept a distance from his pastor's gaffe without losing respect for the anointing and grace on him. He still remembered all the noble deeds of his pastors: the homeless that were housed, how those that were hungry were fed, and how his Pastor's message has changed his life over the years.

Obama's opponents had waited in the wings to capitalize on his pastor's gaffe but after this speech, they lost face. That speech was one of the best during the 2008 campaign and even became a classic. *The New Yorker* columnist, Hendrik Hertzberg, opines that the speech helped elect Obama as the President of the United States.

I can't guarantee that your spiritual leaders and mentors, by their actions and deeds, won't "embarrass" your political campaign. However, it is left to you to decide whether to disown them or acknowledge their investments in your life and make clarifications, where necessary, about where you actually stand on the issue in question.

Yes, you need to crosscheck everything you're taught to ensure they are in line with scriptures and not laced with error.

That was what the Bereans did. You need to know God for yourself. You need to love God and your neighbour. Loving God and your neighbour will solve ALL of the challenges that our world is facing today.

Sleeping and waking up in the church does not qualify you for righteousness; neither does it qualify you for God's grace. A wise man once said that the fact that a cat is sitting on a pillar does not make it a caterpillar. Therefore, genuinely thirst after God.

Whatever the case, you need to honour your spiritual mentors and parents. They serve as cover over you. You need their apostolic covering over your life as you traverse the dangerous political scene. Never allow the activism of the day and the global media to make you lose respect for your spiritual leaders. Remember, they are human just like you and likely to make error. When push comes to shove, when the spiritual arrows of the wicked ones are directed at you, remember that your spiritual leaders will be there for you and not the media or the social media mob.

Lose not Your Confidence
Your membership of God's circle neutralises every diabolical move your opponents makes towards you. Change agents are constantly on the firing line – spiritually and physically. They are harassed to lose confidence. If that fails, assassins are sent after them. Please, lose not your confidence! Real members of

God's circle are immune from the wicked arrow because there is a sure word that the army of change this end time can't be Wounded or Killed! There is a sure word that when they fall on the sword, THEY SHALL NOT BE WOUNDED.[8]And he that touches (them) TOUCHES THE APPLE OF THE EYES OF GOD[9]. Full understanding of these mysteries builds your spiritual muscles that influence your confidence in creating the change in Africa's political terrain.

Start With Small Battles

To build your confidence and spiritual muscle, you need to start with small battles. Diving headlong into any major political battle may crush your confidence. You may get overwhelmed because you have no known records of any battle fought.

> *Build up your confidence by winning small battles irrespective of how insignificant you may think it is.*

More so, God always multiplies the seed you have sown in time past. Nothing can come out of nothing! You can't build something on nothing! Build up your confidence by winning small battles irrespective of how insignificant you may think it is. These little battles sharpen your sword for the bigger battles ahead.

When faced with bigger political battles, you only need to

immediately switch your mental channel to your cabinet and count how many trophies are therein, to find the energy to confront that battle. This would immediately charge your confidence to face the present battle and win. Please note this: Let nobody belittle your so-called small victory. Because, when you allow that to happen, you are setting the stage for a bigger defeat. That small battle may be how you escaped being lynched by some bully when you were in elementary school. It could be how you miraculously escaped being hit by a car when you were young. Those small battles could be those you won when you were in high school and college.

David in the scriptures was faced with the intimidating credentials of Goliath; but he refused to be intimidated by it. He remembered those days in the wilderness when he was keeping his father's sheep and a lion appeared. He killed the lion. It was the same spirit he used to kill Goliath. If David had not practised in the wilderness, his duel with Goliath would have ended in disaster. Therefore, as you get set to storm the political scene, start with small battles so that your faith can be strengthened when faced with bigger battles.

If you don't belittle these small victories, in them lie bigger and global victories of dimensions the world has never seen. Ready to fight bigger battles? Start small. Grow bigger. Never remain stagnant. Never remain on the same spot for a long time. Volunteer more. Work for free. Intern with experienced political organisations and people and before long, you will be playing in the league of political warriors.

Entry into the league of political warriors requires certification in winning at small battles. Without that, it will be practically impossible to fit in for the bigger battles.

THINK!

•*Change makers must be deep spiritually, building their spiritual muscle by communing with the supernatural beyond this physical realm.*

•*Oration without deep spirituality is nothing but nursery rhymes.*

•*When your spiritual muscle is fully grown, you speak deep wisdom.*

•*When positive change makers hear from heaven, supernatural confidence is released to confront any known or unknown obstacle and usher in new politics.*

THINK!

•When your spiritual muscle is fully grown, you speak
with unquenchable confidence that drips with
lots of wits and wisdom.

•Our world needs oracles, not orators.

•Never allow the activism of the day and the global
media to make you lose respect for
your spiritual leaders.

•Build up your confidence by winning small battles
irrespective of how insignificant you may think it is.

THE POWER OF
REPUTATION

CHAPTER 5

THE POWER OF REPUTATION

Vox Populi, Vox Dei is politics; Politics is *Vox Populi, Vox Dei*. The voice of the people is the voice of God.

In politics, everything you do is about people. After God, it is people that determine your destiny in politics. That's the reason every battle cry in any political arena is about people. Therefore, having an acceptable reputation in the eyes of the people cannot be over-emphasised.

In essence, your consistent actions and what people perceive, think, believe or feel about you is your reputation. Though reputation might be flimsy, it plays a big part in politics which is a full contact sport. That's one of the reasons political opponents and foes wrestle one another to a standstill to taint one another's reputation in the eyes of the people. Character is the ultimate but reputation is equally important in politics. The former will be discussed in the next chapter. For now, let's keep our focus on reputation.

As God looks inward to see the contents of the heart (character); so do men look on the outside (reputation). The electorate (because they are human) vote based on emotions, which is often shaped by what they hear, see, touch, etc.

Someone has said that image is everything in politics. There is some truth to that statement, even though I don't totally agree with it. The truth is that in politics, we have seen a dictator rebranded into a democrat. Cases abound of corrupt elements polished into a man of character. What made this happen? Reputation Management did the magic!

Reputation Management

As a reminder, the beliefs or opinions that are generally held about someone or something make up its' reputation. Experts also see reputation as the widespread belief that someone or something has a particular habit or characteristic.

> In essence, your consistent actions and what people perceive, think, believe or feel about you is your reputation.

Reputation can either mar or make any political endeavour. For someone with high and good reputation among the electorate, there is a higher likelihood of getting elected. In contrast, an individual with a damaged or less-than-impressive reputation will likely struggle to get elected by the electorate. The good news is that no matter the state of your reputation right now, it can be managed to expectation.

That said, reputation management is not a stroll in the park. It takes continuous and consistent communication and messaging. Managing one's reputation takes nurturing. It takes planning and strategic thinking. It takes time and energy.

If you have an eye on international, national or local politics, the service of an erudite reputation manager is of utmost essence. When fishing for a reputation manager, bear in mind that you need a well-rounded person. You must engage someone who not only has knowledge of the traditional and new media; but who also understands the principles of strategy, war and battle.

You need someone who understands the trends in local and global politics. You need a reputation manager who is a strategist. You need someone that's dynamic. You need someone with the heart of a lion. A good reputation manager is strategic to shaping your reputation in the eyes of your target audience cum electorates and, by implication, your victory in politics. Reputation managers are 'super-human'. They carry the shield of their principal in difficult terrains, protecting their principal from every attack. They clear the mess created either by commission or omission. If they are not on the offensive, they

> *A good reputation manager is strategic to shaping your reputation in the eyes of your target audience cum electorates and, by implication, your victory in politics.*

are on the defensive for the sake of their principal. I call them burden-bearers.

A reputation manager who knows his worth is always on the offensive and in perpetual crisis mode, even if all look rosy at the moment. S/he is always scanning the terrain to see any booby trap laid ahead for the principal. S/he detects hotspots and diffuses it before it snowballs. The reputation manager is the master of the strategy game. You need one to wade through successfully on the political terrain. And, don't only have a decorative reputation manager; listen to his/her advice. It's why you hired them in the first place.

Reputation in the Digital Age

There is a saying that the evils that men do live long after them. Well, this is especially true in the digital age. Life has been totally transformed in this digital age. People live, work, pay, pray and play online. People bank online. Trade is carried out online. In the future, I believe that state, national and international elections will be conducted online. Essentially, if you can imagine it online, you can get it online.

The online space is an important part of managing your reputation. The reputation an individual has online can easily be carried into the real world. Instances abound in this age, where elections are substantially won and lost online. Though there is a cacophony of discourse online reminiscent of the Tower of Babel; still, the online space is too important to be left alone.

In this section, I will explain how you can manage your reputation successfully in the online space. Strategically, when approaching the online space, it should be treated with all seriousness. Loads of mishaps have been recorded due to sloppiness and ignorance on how to manage the online space. Please understand and know that whatever you don't want to be associated with you in whatever form; don't write it online on any platform whatsoever. Avoid tweeting it. Don't post it. Don't like it. Ensure your comment(s) on status updates can be referenced without leaving you feeling any sense of shame. Have it in mind that your status updates online represent you and your brand. I often tell people: show me your social media timelines and I will tell you who you are.

> *Essentially, if you can imagine it online, you can get it online.*

Sterling Online Reputation

To successfully lead change on the political scene this end time, you must have a good reputation both online and offline. Your activities offline will reflect on your personality and reputation online. The two goes *paripassu*. One can't be left for the other. When you decide to seek elective office or be a player in whatever form on the political scene, expect that your name will constantly be queried on search engines by your supporters and foes alike. People would constantly want to get updates, information, dirt, etc., that are related to you in whatever form. That's the reason you must take seriously your reputation online.

Before setting out to clean up your online space, please know that the online space is constantly changing. The big search engines are constantly tweaking their algorithm in order to discourage people from gaming their system. However, the good news is that there are fundamental principles that will fit every algorithm change of search engines.

First, do a Google search for your name regularly, in order to know what people are seeing and saying about you. You may think it does not

> *Ensure you're heard where the electorate and your target audience hang out.*

matter, but it does. In this digital age, decisions are made based on what people read online and the disadvantage of this is that, you may not be there to give them your version of the story.

Don't be satisfied with results on the first page alone. Go deeper into the second and third pages of the search engines. To take charge of your web results, you need to populate the web with your deliberate content as much as possible.

Create a blog and write interesting articles that reflect your brand. Endeavour to write and attain the status of a thought-leader in your industry. Make your views known on issues trending in the country. Ensure you're heard where the electorate and your target audience hang out. Enlist the services of your friends, fans and allies to give wings to your contents across the web by sharing it heavily.

In a bid to be where your audience is, ensure that you're not stretching yourself too thin. Know where the electorate are online and give them interesting and relevant content. Have a respectable presence on leading social media platforms. For those platforms that are not popular, colonise your name there. As your fame grows, constantly do an audit of your name online to ensure someone is not using it to fleece people or for other nefarious activities.

Also, taking hold of your online presence means that you secure your full name as a domain name (yourfirstandlastname.com) early. The beauty of domain names is that they are in different variants. There are: .com; .net; .org; .me;.xyz, etc. If .com is not available, ensure you get the other ones. But by all means, ensure you have your name registered as a domain before cyber-squatters, or your opponents, get a hold of it. In the run-up to the 2016 presidential election, Donald Trump registered more than 3,600 domain names relating to his personal and business brands.

You may not need to go the whole hog like Donald Trump, but you need to be proactive about the way your brand will be projected online.

The stronger your brand online and offline become; the costlier it will become to get your preferred domain names if it's not done in the days of obscurity.

The Power of a Personal Profile

In addition to the content that you have developed to crowd the web, when you write a personal profile online, you dictate to a large extent what will be written about you. People may read about you before meeting you in person. So, take advantage of that to shape people's perception of you.

> *Leverage on your strengths and opportunities. Use every known avenue to project positively your strengths and opportunities while working to turn your weaknesses and threats to opportunities.*

Ensure that you tweak your profile differently on different platforms in order to give the search engine an opportunity to pick up the different variants. Also ensure that you write your profile in third person. The search engine considers profiles written that way as more credible to be included in search results. Ensure your written profiles vary in length and content, depending on the platforms where it will be posted. For example, instead of writing:*"I am a journalist and media strategist with rich experience in the media industry..."*

Consider writing it this way: *"Samuel O. Adeyemi is a journalist and media strategist with rich experience in the media industry..."*

The second example is the better way to write your profile because it ranks better on search engines, which will help your reputation. In your profile, include the best and most interesting details of your life. Leave the other less interesting details for your memoirs. A profile is not the place to tell the world about the fifty years of your existence. Simply give the most important details that will improve your reputation and ensure that it is updated often.

> *When you ride on your strengths, your brand and reputation will exude acceptance.*

Building a Strong Reputation
By now, you understand what reputation means and the power of your reputation. So, how do you build your reputation and become valuable in the eyes of your target audience and the electorate? For starters, do a SWOT analysis on yourself. SWOT means Strength, Weakness, Opportunity and Threat. In doing a SWOT analysis, you must be truthful to yourself in order to get the best out of that exercise. If you are entirely truthful when detailing the SWOT analysis on yourself, you will be confronted with facts that will either make or mar your political career.

Leverage on your strengths and opportunities. Use every known avenue to project positively your strengths and opportunities while working to turn your weaknesses and threats to opportunities.

Be careful not to wallow in self-pity because of the weaknesses and threats in your reputation. Work on your threats and weaknesses and as I mentioned earlier, by all means amplify your strengths. Ride on your strengths. Make one or two of them your centre-piece. When push comes to shove, your strengths are what will speak for you as you work on your challenges. Through your weaknesses and threats, you can channel out the opportunities to explore to change the public attitude toward and perception of you. This is where you need a strategic communicator to work with. When you ride on your strengths, your brand and reputation will exude acceptance.

Here are other ways to build your reputation:

1.   *Have A Message And Always Stay On Message*

To be taken seriously in the new political order of Africa, you must have an ideology and virtues. You must have what you stand for. We're in the era of politics with principles. If you stand for nothing, you will fall for everything. Let your yay be yay, and nay be nay.

A politician without a message in the new Africa will soon be washed away by the waves. It is imperative that you understand what resonates with your audience and tweak your message to fit them.

When there is need to tweak your message to fit the present reality, ensure that you're really convinced that's the right path to take and not just responding to pressure in order to "feel among and belong". Ensure that any message or ideology you're projecting at any point in time is consistent with your belief system.

2.   *Take A Helicopter View of Issues*

The fact that you hold dear your view doesn't mean you should not see the world from others' point of view. Always argue only after considering both sides of the issue. There is no point arguing and holding tight to your views because you have refused to see the other person's point of view. This only leads to avoidable rancour, wasting time, energy and material resources in the process. When you take a helicopter view, you will be objective and leave out every form of bias in your intervention, be it in written or in spoken words. People that take such a view of issues and consider other people are always loved and have an acceptable reputation.

3.   *Be Knowledgeable*

Ignorance is a disease. It repels people. People who know a little bit about everything often have a good reputation.

What knowing something about everything does is that it makes you a rounded person and broadens your world view. You will understand the complexity of human relations and that will help you to situate issues, then understand and manage people appropriately.
Go for knowledge. Knowledge is light. When you have light, people gravitate towards you. Nonetheless, be careful; don't just be bookish. Be knowledgeable and apply what you have learnt in a proactive and strategic manner.

4. *Take Advantage of PR Opportunities*

One of the fastest ways to gain reputation and national prominence is to leverage on Public Relations (PR) opportunities. Many of the famous people we know today leveraged heavily on PR to get known.

Media coverage can do more than build awareness and credibility. Never take for granted any opportunity to be featured in the media; you never can tell who will be watching, listening or reading. Media travels faster than any place you can imagine to visit – except of course dreamland.

A mention in an obscure blog can spell doom just as much as a feature in a prominent blog can take your reputation a number of notches higher. The difference is that the probability of the former is higher. Same thing applies for a feature in a newspaper.

You build your reputation when you get involved in activities that will engender press coverage. PR is less costly if done the right way. Lend your voice to what's happening in your community, country

> *Saying the truth may not sound appealing when you are going through the crisis; but at the end of the day, you will thank God you stuck to the truth.*

and continent; write an article for publication in newspapers/blogs; phone-in to program and display your knowledge/expertise, etc.

5.   *Have a Rapid Response Team*

To build your reputation, you need a Rapid Response Team that will be on the lookout for any red flags that could taint your reputation. The team has to be proactive and always on the offensive.
The task of this team is to continuously guard your reputation and fight to keep your reputation intact.

6.   *Proactively Design A Coordinated Communication Plan*

Having a coordinated media plan will help your Rapid Response Team to know what to do. It is a proactive tool rather than a reactive one that distinguishes successful politicians from the not-so-successful.

Therefore, sit with your consultants and media aides to fashion out a strong communication plan that will not only be strategic in focus but be detailed enough for tactical plans to guard, build, grow and nurture your reputation.

7.   *Dress The Way You Want to be Addressed*

It sounds like cliché right? The fact is that humans look at the outward appearance while God looks upon the heart. The way you dress always dictates the way people will address you.
I have attended a national event before where an incumbent national President of Nigeria's trade union was "bounced" at the entrance. Also, a former governor of a popular state was denied entrance at the same event. Why? Those manning the entrance didn't consider them appropriately dressed for the occasion; after all, other attendees at the same event were better dressed, as befitting of their status. However, these two gentlemen were later allowed entrance when other guests at the event saw and identified them.

The whole idea here is to dress the part. No need to dress

in a flamboyant manner. Dress moderately. Dress sensibly. Dress the way you want to be perceived. Dressing the part will positively affect your self-esteem, your confidence level and hence, your reputation.

Crisis Communication

When your reputation runs into stormy waters in the course of your political career, do not despair. There is a way out. With strategic thinking and planning, you can manage the situation adequately and come out sparkling. Your watchword during a time of crisis is "truth". Never sacrifice the truth for anything. Resist the temptation to spin the issue. Say the truth and expect the truth to set you free. Saying the truth may not sound appealing when you are going through the crisis; but at the end of the day, you will thank God you stuck to the truth.

Before crisis strikes, prep your team for any eventualities. Simulate any known situation that may occur and designate roles for each member of your team in such scenarios. In constituting your team, it is important that you have a lawyer present. However, ensure that the lawyer doesn't take the final decision. The way a lawyer thinks is usually different from the way a PR professional would think. In times of crisis, a thoroughbred PR professional on your team will take a cue from best practices by telling it all, telling it fast and telling the truth.

THINK!

•*A good reputation manager is strategic to shaping your reputation in the eyes of your target audience cum electorates and, by implication, your victory in politics.*

•*Essentially, if you can imagine it online, you can get it online.*

•*Ensure you're heard where the electorate and your target audience hang out.*

•*Use every known avenue to project positively your strengths and opportunities while working to turn your weaknesses and threats to opportunities.*

THINK!

•When you ride on your strengths, your brand and reputation will exude acceptance.

•Saying the truth may not sound appealing when you are going through the crisis; but at the end of the day , you will thank God you stuck to the truth.

THE POWER OF
CHARACTER

CHAPTER 6

THE POWER OF CHARACTER

Beyond branding, beyond packaging, beyond the surface, beyond the consciousness of the prying eyes of traditional and new media; beyond friends' and fans' applause and beyond the foregoing reputation management recommendations are my definite definitions of character.

Character is your inner being which is very difficult for humans to see easily, but blatantly visible to your creator. How you react in your closet when no one is watching is a definite pointer to your character.
Nevertheless, no matter how much you try to conceal and "rebrand" it, your character will be revealed to the world in due course. Character is like a shadow - you can't run away from it. Character is a raging inferno; no matter how long or how fiercely it is suppressed, in due time, it will blow open.

Character is not a "fashionable" topic among politicians in Africa belonging to the old order. Even in our educational system, it is discussed in hush tones, while competence gets the louder acclaim. Don't get me wrong, competence is needed. In fact, to function in this new era of politics, one must have a good blend of competence and character. Competence and character are needed to make in roads into the new political scene of Africa. As we inch closer to the new way of playing politics in the new Africa, character will be the one of the biggest game changers.

Without character, your political vision in this new era will be like a visually-appealing pot of stew with scintillating aroma, but without commensurate excellence in the taste department. Anyone deficient in character has no place in this new era of politics. In this new era of politics in Africa, without character, you will be nobody.

> *As we inch closer to the new way of playing politics in the new Africa, character will be the one of the biggest game changers.*

In politics, your character is crucial to your success, but so is your reputation. The former is inherent while the latter is outward. Media gurus can manage the reputation of politicians but it is difficult – if not impossible – to manage character. Reputation can be polished; character can't. That's the reason why character must be consciously built and strengthened. Without strength of character, the politicians in the new Africa will discover that their ambition is "dead on arrival!"

Therefore, in the days of obscurity, consciously and

deliberately build your character. Be in a perpetual state of panting after your Creator. Building character is not a hundred-meter dash; it is a long distance race that requires persistence, determination and strength. You build your character by being true to your God. Be true to your conscience. Be true to your family and friends. Consciously be a man and woman of your words. Say what you mean; mean what you say. Remember it is only a solid character that births strong social capital.

> *In this new era of politics in Africa, without character, you will be nobody.*

Without character, you're bankrupt!
We all know that competence and character are in short supply around the world. However, once you have both in satisfactory quantity, the demand on you will be huge. Doors of nations will open and unlimited opportunities will follow you. After all, even crooks and frauds are looking for sincere people they can trust with parts of their activities.

While many will jostle and struggle for leadership positions in the new Africa, those with high dose of character and competence will be freely given responsibilities without them requesting for it. It will come on a platter of gold.

Reputation and Character
When it comes to choosing between your reputation and character; please choose your character. That's what will set you apart.

In the coming days, there will be lots of qualified people; but people of character will be few and far between. Character will be an aroma that will draw people and fortunes to you. A combination of character, reputation and competence is a dynamo. Go for that combination. It is possible to have all three in large quantity.

Reputation is fleeting. Character is solid.
Even at the cost of your political career, choose character over reputation. Sooner or later, you will be vindicated and your virtues will catapult you beyond your widest vision and imagination in politics.

In the words of Heraclitus, "Character is destiny." Alan Simpson said, "If you have integrity, nothing else matters. If you don't have integrity, nothing else matters." Erwin C. Hargrove also argues that a leader must have character: "The statesman does not invoke moral absolutes to cowed or deferential citizens. Rather, he must evoke those values and beliefs that citizens implicitly hold and apply them to the solution of particular problems."

A solid character can withstand any onslaught by political opponents, detractors, and foes alike.

Having advised four American presidents, author and communication expert, David Gergen, in his bestselling book,

New Thinking New Politics

Eyewitness to Power: The Essence of Leadership Nixon to Clinton,
asserts that "trust is still the coin of the realm of politics."

The character of a leader determines the decisions and
judgment s/he makes. Political leadership, and any form of
leadership for that matter, is about judgment. It's about taking
decisions on what's right or wrong by the second. Therefore, it
follows that our character will in no small measure shape our
judgement of issues and situations as
it affects those we lead in our
organisations and our country.

> *Character will decide
> the colour of your
> leadership.
> Always remember: No
> character, No trust.*

Dr. Billy Graham admonishes in
his autobiography, *Just As I Am*:
"True greatness is not measured by
the headlines a person commands or
the wealth he or she accumulates. The
inner character of a person – the undergirding moral and
spiritual values and commitment – is the true measure of lasting
greatness." Character will decide the colour of your leadership.
Always remember: No character, No trust.

HOW TO BUILD SOLID CHARACTER
Building solid character is a major task for would-be politicians
in the new Africa. Your character is your life. If you will make
any meaningful impact in politics, take time to build your
character.

A solid character can withstand any onslaught by political opponents, detractors, and foes alike. The following will show you how to have a solid and unassailable character:

Be Accountable
Accountability ensures that you are subjected to the leadership of someone or a group of people who can chastise you and tell you the truth which no one can tell you. A man or woman who is not accountable to anyone is a dangerous being. That person can do and undo. The person act on a whim to his own detriment when there is an accountability system in place, discretion will be in abundant supply.

> *When choosing those you will be accountable to, have in mind that age should not be a major criteria. Let wisdom, knowledge, values and discretion be the major criteria.*

The challenge of young people is that everyone wants to be a lord unto himself/herself. No one wants to be subjected to another person. This is a time bomb waiting to explode. Absolute independence is a dangerous thing. Run away from it. Having an accountability system in place will save you from going astray from your core values. When choosing those you will be accountable to, have in mind that age should not be a major criteria. Let wisdom, knowledge, values and discretion be the major criteria. Ensure that those you are considering to be accountable to have the same core values as yours.

100

Have a Mentor

A wise man once said that you can either learn through a mentor or through mistakes. Learning through mistakes is very costly. It can cost you your political career and aspiration. On the other hand, learning through a mentor will accelerate your steps through life. Mentorship gives you a lift. Mentorship moulds you.

Ensure you have a mentor. Your mentor will serve as a check on your actions and inactions. Mentoring is one of the sure ways to build a solid character as every true protégé is subject to the moulding of the mentor.
A good mentor moulds the character of the protégé to conform to acceptable and divine standards.

> *Mentoring is one of the sure ways to build a solid character as every true protégé is subject to the moulding of the mentor.*

Be Sincere With Yourself

Being sincere with yourself means that you're absolutely honest with God and man. You don't camouflage your weaknesses. You understand your weaknesses and make cogent plans to work on the flaws without giving unnecessary excuses. You own up to your shortcomings and accept responsibility for your flaws.

Ask God for Help

Resolutions, determinations and willpower are limited when building a solid character. The help of God is needed in this quest. It is only through the help of God that a solid character can be built and sustained in a dangerous political terrain like Africa.

When you're humble enough to ask God for help, you will surely have solid character. With character and competence, Africa needs you.

THINK!

- As we inch closer to the new way of playing politics in the new Africa, character will be the one of the biggest game changers.

- In this new era of politics in Africa, without character, you will be nobody.

- Without character, you're bankrupt!

- Reputation is fleeting. Character is solid.

- Character will decide the colour of your leadership.

- Always remember: No character, No trust.

THINK!

•*A solid character can withstand any onslaught by political opponents, detractors, and foes alike.*

•*When choosing those you will be accountable to, have in mind that age should not be a major criteria. Let wisdom, knowledge, values and discretion be the major criteria.*

•*Mentoring is one of the sure ways to build a solid character as every true protégé is subject to the moulding of the mentor.*

•*With character and competence, Africa needs you.*

PART 2

NEW POLITICS

There is a path where no falcon's eyes have seen.
There is a place the stiffest lion has not trodden.[10]

THE HEART BIGGER THAN ANY
POLITICAL PARTY

CHAPTER 7

THE HEART BIGGER THAN ANY POLITICAL PARTY

The prevailing reputation notwithstanding, politics is a noble calling. As democracy spreads around the world, becoming a vehicle for peaceful change of government, politics is serving as one of the fastest avenues to effect change, touch lives and shape the history of nations and great nations. Any group of people who have access to political power have been known to dictate the pace of the socio-economic prosperity of wherever they hold sway.

That is why it is of outmost importance that men and women of sterling character, sincerity, competence and with a heart for service invade the political space and change it for the better. Politics is too important to be left in the hands of charlatans. "One of the penalties for refusing to participate in politics is that you end up being governed by your inferiors,"Plato once said.

Of Political Parties
In modern politics, the political party is a vehicle that drives the political visions and ambitions of politicians. The political party

system has smoothened out the process of choosing and nominating political candidates vying for elective positions. With people exiting and joining a political party, tales of friends becoming foes; foes becoming friends; dictators turning democrats; strange bed fellows seen smiling and "uniting" towards the same cause, etc., all abound.

However, in this new dispensation of new politics, those that will shape the history of Africa for good are those whose hearts are bigger than any political party. These are people whose allegiance is to God and the country alone and not a band of power-hungry folks who hide under the banner of a political party to hold a man/woman on assignment hostage. Your motto as a politician should be God and country first, followed by your political party. If you have a heart bigger than any political party, you will take over governance at every level without the support of any cabal and clique. You will remain relevant in all dispensations.

> *Your motto as a politician should be God and country first, followed by your political party.*

Don't be unnecessarily partisan all in the name of party loyalty. Say the truth no matter whose ox is gored. Elevate your thoughts beyond the mundane. Think like statesmen; because while some politicians and voters think about the next election, statesmen think about the next generation. As an advocate of the new politics, you're after the well-being of the next generation.

You must be able to discern the wolves in sheep's clothing. You must be able to spot the "emergency democrats". If we truly want transformation in all spheres of life as a nation, country and continent, we must choose to see the big picture and eschew petty politics, because it only leads to pettiness. It leads to a petty economy. It leads to the provision of petty solutions to the myriad of challenges facing our continent.

> *You must be able to discern the wolves in sheep's clothing. You must be able to spot the "emergency democrats".*

When we have a heart bigger than any party, we will assess candidates based on their own merit, rather than be narrow-minded, basing our choice on tribe, ethnicity and religion. As an active political player in the new politics, we should endeavour to vote CHARACTER and COMPETENCE; vote for INDIVIDUAL, not the POLITICAL PARTY.

As a strong observer of public issues, I can confidently tell you that merits abound on either side of the aisle. This is however not a license to go off the hook and disregard party rules. Party loyalty still has its place. But when that rules conflict with your values, that of your creator and the people God has sent you to, you have got to react. To successfully have a heart bigger than any political affiliation, you must be filled with the spirit of wisdom. The spirit of wisdom sets you apart. With it, you can easily discern between good and evil; truth and falsehood; etc.

When you're filled with the spirit of wisdom, people of all ages will seek after you. Your views will be easily accepted across the aisle.

Of State of Origin & Ethnic Affiliation

The hearts of ethnic jingoists are rarely big. Everything they see is shrunk to fit into their small world view. Hearts not bigger than states of origin will go nowhere; it has no place in the new politics. Therefore, think like a statesman. Judge issues based on its merits and not how it favours your ethnic group and place of origin. This means you have to be fair and just. A lot of people see themselves as being part of their ethnic group first before being part of humanity. Go against that and attempt to see yourself as part of humanity first before being part of your ethnic group.

For those advocating for a new politics, the scourge of political "godfatherism" is one of those battles that need to be won.

Doing this makes you rise above every limiting tradition of your ethnic group that is holding down the progress of your country and continent. In the continent of Africa, there are so many limiting traditions and practices which will hinder the emergence of new thinking and the new politics we earnestly crave for. No matter how anointed you are, if you're unduly sold out to the traditions in your state of origin or ethnic group, it won't be long before the burning zeal to create a paradigm shift will be quenched. By divine appointment, if you determine to stand for the truth and progress, you will be like Daniel in the scriptures who couldn't be side-lined by any government.

The Scourge of Political godfatherism

At this nascent stage of the democratic experiment in Africa, the will of the people is often bypassed, a phenomenon which is antithetical to the very nature of democracy. This subversion often finds fervour in the activities of those who

> *Never put your trust in any godfather. Let God be your real godfather.*

constitute themselves as kingmakers and godfathers in every political contest. These people, by the nature of their influence and power, would determine who wins the political contest without regard to the wishes of the people.

And when they get their way by imposing a stooge in government, the stooge is subject to their dictates and wishes. For those advocating for a new politics, the scourge of political "godfatherism" is one of those battles that need to be won. Respect the elders, take the advice of the elders but weigh it against the word of God. If it doesn't fit with the word of God, discard it very fast! Never put your trust in any godfather. Let God be your real godfather. Very soon, all those parading themselves as godfathers would run to you for wisdom, spiritual cover and direction.

If God before you, which godfather can be against you? Respect all men; but fear no man! Above all, respect God. Fear God.

Personal Transformation

Transformation starts from within. It does not start from the outside. If we truly want to have new politics and a new nation, we must start advocating for people to do the right things.

> *Except we change as individuals, nothing will change for us as a nation and continent. We must be advocates of personal transformation.*

Except we change as individuals, nothing will change for us as a nation and continent. We must be advocates of personal transformation. It is first within before the outside. Fast tracking of infrastructure around the African continent must be preceded by the restructuring of the minds of the people of Africa. Any nation whose citizens are not developed from the inside can never have development on the outside.

This therefore behoves on we the advocates of new politics the responsibility of understanding that a lot of work lies ahead of us. We must re-orientatethe people. We must educate the people. We must tell the people what the right things to do are. National orientation across every African continent must be more focused, planned and strategic. The average African must be helped to understand that we have to create, create and create first. Enough of wanton consumption; we must create whatever we need!

112

THINK!

•*Your motto as a politician should be God and country first, followed by your political party.*

•*You must be able to discern the wolves in sheep's clothing. You must be able to spot the "emergency democrats".*

•*For those advocating for a new politics, the scourge of political "godfatherism" is one of those battles that need to be won.*

•*Never put your trust in any godfather. Let God be your real godfather.*

THINK!

•*Except we change as individuals, nothing will change*
for us as a nation and continent.
We must be advocates of personal transformation.

•*National orientation across every African*
continent must be more focused,
planned and strategic.

THE NEW
POLITICS

CHAPTER 8

THE NEW POLITICIAN

We are in the days where men stronger than the sword will emerge on the political scene. We are in the days when men like horses shall bestride mightily the political scene of Africa. We are in the days when men who have vowed to see the end of evil and corruption will take centre stage on the political scene of Africa.

These strange politicians shall be working and walking in strange dimensions of grace; that their opponents can't but be silenced by their level of results. These new politicians are compassionate; have pity on the downtrodden; they love their people genuinely; they have a tender heart. Their confidence level is high because they know that he that is within them is greater than he that is in the world.

They have what former British Prime Minister, John Major, calls the "political nose to detect the political wind."
What are the other elements that will set you apart as a new politician?

Power of the Stagecraft
As a politician in this new dispensation, you must understand

116

that oratory power is a mandatory. When you are given the microphone, the earth must shake under your feet at the sound of your voice.

Your voice must be full of power. Therefore, ensure you do not speak vain words. Speak words of power. Speak words of wisdom. Speak creatively. Speak to confound the opposition. It is only after mastering your voice and words that you can master the stage. Make the stage your friend. Embrace the stage. Never be intimidated by the stage. Understand the power that can be unleashed on the stage if properly harnessed.

The stage may not necessarily be a physical structure elevated above the ground. Your stage could be the sofa on which you're sitting to record your remarks on video. Your stage may be those short clips that go on social media and other new media. Your stage may be words you're scribbling down for publication. In essence, anytime you have the opportunity of pushing your ideas into the public space, realise that you're mounting a soapbox to influence people and elevate your brand beyond the reach of those opposed to your ideals.

In essence, anytime you have the opportunity of pushing your ideas into the public space, realise that you're mounting a soapbox to influence people and elevate your brand beyond the reach of those opposed to your ideals.

Political Intelligence

Navigating through the political configuration of any nation demands intelligence, interest and experience. Surviving and thriving in your political environment demands that you have knowledge that will set you apart. Spirituality is no substitute for knowledge. Neither is knowledge a substitute for spirituality. The two are needed to make you succeed in this era. In fact, lack of any of these will torpedo your political career.

> *Spirituality is no substitute for knowledge. Neither is knowledge a substitute for spirituality. The two are needed to make you succeed in this era. In fact, lack of any of these will torpedo your political career.*

You can't change what you don't know about. Therefore, you must develop your political intelligence to ensure you get elected and stay elected. (There is a difference between being elected and staying elected. Some elected officials are impeached and shown the exit door because of political naivety.) A high level of political intelligence makes you an "expert" in your local politics. You can outwit the wittiest of politicians in your locality when you have a high level of political intelligence.

The "powerful" elements who have pitched their tents around your political area of influence can be surmounted through intelligence. You need to know the political godfathers around you but don't in anyway kowtow to them. Know the voting blocs so as to carve an appropriate political strategy to capture them into your net. To build political intelligence, have the following in mind:

I.   *Interest:* Interest is important in building political intelligence. What you're not interested in, you cannot attract. In other words, your political intelligence is developed when you're actively interested in happenings around you, political or otherwise.

      In this context, interest means active participation and involvement to make things happen. It also means detecting the "political hotspots" around you and finding ways to plugin.

ii.   *Experience:* This may sound like a catch22 for new entrants into politics who are eager to quickly make their impact felt. Catch22 because to navigate successfully on the political terrain, there is need to have political experience; and there are not many known ways to have political experience without active participation in politics.

      The good news for those just making their entrance into politics is that their learning curve can be shortened and they can gain experience through active participation, studying the history and political strategy books, studying political trends in their locality, studying the interrelation between psychology, political science and human relations. The keyword here is "study". When you study, you accelerate your steps in the political field.

iii.   *Campaign Intelligence*
For the electorate to know you and commit their destinies into your hands, they need to know and hear you. This is where campaigning comes in. A botched campaign is synonymous with a botched political career.

Making the most of available options is crucial to passing your message successfully to the voters. Leverage on technology to reach the target audience but NEVER push aside the knocking on doors of voters. Personal contacts of voters by the candidates is still of utmost importance.

Leverage on technology to reach the target audience but NEVER push aside the knocking on doors of voters. Personal contacts of voters by the candidates is still of utmost importance.

Political science researchers have noted that ground game is necessary during the campaign. They asserted that knocking on voters' doors "can increase turnout by nearly 10%, and effective phone calls can encourage an additional 4% of voters to head to the polls."

120

Create every "excuse" to make contact with voters and share your message. Create listening tours before you start rolling out your ideologies to voters. Refine your message to fit the different voting blocs in your community. Attend town hall meetings and prepare adequately for debates against your opponent. During the campaign, always stay on the offensive because being on the defensive may be dangerous to your political quest.

Retail Politics
Technological breakthrough in mass communication should not stop you from making personal contact with voters. Having a personal relationship with voters in smaller units is what retail politics is about. Ensuring that voters, wherever they maybe, have a feel of the candidate up-close is the nucleus of retail politics all over the world.

Organise People
Your organisation of people will determine if you will win the ground game or lose to your opponent. People are vital in translating your overall strategy into tactical actions that lead to victory at the polls. Organise people into teams. Employ full-time staff. Have volunteers. Engage those that will be willing to go on road-shows with you. Without properly organising people, and inspiring them, you're likely to misfire in your political career.

Entry Polls
An entry poll is the survey of voters before they cast their votes

in the election. It is directly related to the opinion poll. Having your team or expert conduct an entry poll for you may save you avoidable heartache. Depending on the laws of your country, you may be able to, as a result of the entry polls, quickly tweak your strategy and message in order to convince voters to vote for you before they eventually head to the polls.

Exit Polls

To adequately prepare for your next political duel, pay attention to the exit and entry polls. The exit poll is defined as a representation of voters' voting patterns after they leave the polling stations.

THINK!

•Anytime you have the opportunity of pushing
your ideas into the public space,
realise that you're mounting a soapbox
to influence people and elevate your brand
beyond the reach of those opposed to your ideals.

•Spirituality is no substitute for knowledge. Neither
is knowledge a substitute for spirituality.
The two are needed to make you
succeed in this era. In fact, lack of any
of these will torpedo your political career.

•Leverage on technology to reach the target audience
but NEVER push aside the knocking on doors of voters.
Personal contacts of voters by the
candidates is still of utmost importance.

THE POWER OF
EMOTION

CHAPTER 9

THE POWER OF EMOTION

Never underestimate the power of emotions to make or mar your political career. Sometimes, it is not the most logical arguments that sink into the hearts of the electorate. Rather, it is the most emotional argument that does. It is therefore necessary to master the art of crafting and delivering sincere and emotional laden speeches that appeal to the electorate. Of what good would it be when you have good plans couched in logical nuances which cannot connect with the hearts of those who will grant you the permission to lead them? Examples abound around the world of how politicians have used emotions to their advantage in their quest for political office.

With a barrage of unfavourable opinion polls and an unorthodox presidential campaign, President Donald Trump created an upset in the US political history by becoming the 45th President of the United States through the perfect use of emotions. You may argue rightly that President Trump insulted his way and trampled upon some people's sensibility into the presidency, but the fact remains that he spoke the minds of millions of Americans who felt disenchanted and left behind in the American dream.

Though his private and public life may reflect that of a liberal, his speeches and promises on the campaign trail tallies with the yearnings of the conservative movement. Researchers at The Ohio State University revealed that Trump's emotional laden speeches on the campaign trail landed him the presidency.

It is therefore necessary to master the art of crafting and delivering sincere and emotional laden speeches that appeal to the electorate.

"The Donald speaks mirrors the average conversation - which makes supporters believe he is an honest outsider," so says David Clementson, a Ph.D. candidate at The Ohio State University. "Trump's emotionally-charged language is exactly why his followers want him in the White House, as it makes him seem more trustworthy. This type of behavior from a presidential candidate is only acceptable during times of economic hardships, as voters feel it reflects their own fears and uncertainties of the future."

The research result from The Ohio State University continues: "During economic stability, voters want a candidate that can practices restraint when it comes to what they say." The research also indicates that if a political candidate is speaking to the times, he will be viewed "as more trustworthy".

In other words, "If you use low-intensity language in stable circumstances, you're more trustworthy. Conversely, if you use high-intensity language in exigent circumstances, you're more trustworthy."

Examples abound around the world of how politicians have used emotions to their advantage in their quest for political office.

This research was reported in *Daily Mail* of March 21, 2016. The paper reported that the study was conducted during the 2012 election with 300 students from the University of Miami, who held varying political ideologies. Similarly, Drew Westen, Professor of psychology and psychiatry at Emory University, in his book, *The Political Brain: The Role of Emotion in Deciding the Fate of the Nation*, states that: "The idea of the mind as a cool calculator that makes decisions by weighing the evidence bears no relation to how the brain works and when political candidates assume voters dispassionately make decisions based on issues, they lose.

"In politics, when reason and emotion collide, emotion invariably wins. Elections are decided in the market place of emotions, a marketplace filled with values, images, analogies, moral sentiments and moving oratory, in which logic plays only a supporting role."

Prof. Westen asserts that three things determine how people vote:

(i)   their feelings toward the parties and their principles,

(ii)   their feelings toward the candidates, and, if they haven't decided by then,

(iii)   their feelings toward the candidates' policy positions.

In July 2017, a video by Jeff King, an expert in Process Communication Model (PCM), surfaced online. The video explained why Hillary Clinton – despite having a more robust and humane campaign message-lost to Donald Trump in the 2016 US presidential election. In the video, King asserts that Hillary only spoke to "one personality type. And that was logic." He notes that Hillary "perceives the world through thoughts. And she speaks a lot of logic."

According to King, though the fact checkers were on the side of Hillary during the debate, "I was screaming at the TV (that) it doesn't matter because she was only speaking through logic and discounting about 75% (of the voting population)." In an article published on MySA website, Renita Coleman, an associate professor of journalism in the Moody College of Communication at the University of Texas, also argues in favor of emotion during electioneering.

She writes: "Voters don't like to acknowledge that they use their emotions more than logical reasoning when deciding whom to elect as leader of the free world. Yet that is exactly what happens — voters use their emotions to select the candidates they support. "My colleague and I studied this very thing in the past three U.S. presidential elections and found that emotions were at least as important, and sometimes more important, than voters' rational assessments of a politician.

"The way a candidate makes voters feel, specifically angry, afraid, hopeful and proud, has a huge influence on political opinions and ultimately for whom they vote. But as long as emotion is in the forefront, logic is less likely to take over."

Let's bring this discussion to Nigeria, in a back to back election of 2011 and 2015, emotion reigns supreme in Nigeria's political firmaments. Dr. Goodluck Jonathan was perceived as being marginalized and shielded from excrcising presidential powers by the cabal around his ailing boss, President Umaru Yaradua. This perception galvanized the whole nation to force the national assembly to adopt the doctrine of necessity and installed Jonathan as the Acting President.

After the eventual death of Yaradua and on the occasion of the declaration of his candidacy for the PDP presidential primaries on 18th September, 2010, President Jonathan played his cards well by striking a chord among Nigerians by narrating how he had "no shoes", promising a "a breath of fresh air".

He said: "In my early days in school, I had no shoes, no school bags. I carried my books in my hands but never despaired; no car to take me to school but I never despaired.

"There were days I had only one meal but I never despaired. I walked miles and crossed rivers to school every day but I never despaired. Didn't have power, didn't have generators, studied with lanterns but I never despaired."

He spoke emotionally about how the challenges and poverty majority of Nigerians were experiencing are not alien to him. He was elected.

In 2015, the then candidate of the All Progressive Congress (APC), General Muhammed Buhari, paid Dr. Goodluck Jonathan back in his own "emotional coin."

General Buhari claimed he had no money to buy the nomination form of his party. He vigorously identified with the challenges of Nigerians. He had strong emotional ties with majority of Nigerians who were dissatisfied with the performance of President Jonathan's government. In the eyes of General Buhari's supporters, he can do no wrong. During the brouhaha following his school leaving certificate, some supporters even postulated that if General Buhari presented a utility bill in place of his certificate, they would still vote for him.

He skipped the presidential debate. His supporters stuck with him. His strategists understood that Nigerians were fed up with

Jonathan. It was anybody but Jonathan. He therefore promised "Change". The supporters believed him.

Any attempt by the Jonathan's government to task him to give specifics about his programs and what the "change" battle cry entail was viewed by supporters as a form of harassment. He won.

Emotional Home truth

Truth is, emotion works. As you get set to change the political landscape of Africa, ensure you couch your messages in emotion. Refine your messages to meet the very needs of the people.

Note that this is not a license to lie. It is simply a charge for you to master the art of emotional message and present your message to the people. Sincere and emotional laden speeches are great combinations appeal to the electorate. With God on your side, your message will surely resonates in the minds of the people. Never underestimate the power of emotion over logic in political communication.

THINK!

•*Sometimes, it is not the most logical arguments
that sink into the hearts of the electorate.
Rather, it is the most emotional argument that does.*

•*Of what good would it be when you have good
plans couched in logical nuances which cannot
connect with the hearts of those who will
grant you the permission to lead them?*

•*Truth is, emotion works.*

•*As you get set to change the political landscape of
Africa, ensure you couch your messages in emotion.*

•*Refine your messages to meet the very
needs of the people.*

ELECTION
DAY

CHAPTER 10

ELECTION DAY

T he culmination of electioneering, campaigns and political strategy deployment is the result at the polls. That result can only come to full manifestation on Election Day, before and after the polls and when the results start to trickle in. Instead of moving from anxiety to worry and anticipation, what do you need to do on Election Day?

Rely On Your Field Agents
In some developing countries of Africa where an election is a do-or-die affair, restrictions are often placed on movement. It is therefore imperative for anyone vying for elective office in that situation to rely on accredited field and poll agents who are allowed to move freely and stay at the polling stations and collation centres. Ensure that your agents are properly trained. An improperly trained polling agent may cause a mishap for any candidate in an election, because most elections are rigged at the collation centre.

It takes an eagle-eyed and loyal agent to stand firm and stop any "robbery" that may have been planned to take place. A properly trained agent is expected to be on alert and on constant lookout for any anomaly in order to promptly call the attention of the election officials to it.

Leverage Technology

In this age and time, leveraging technology is non-negotiable. In politics, technology can leapfrog you ahead of your competition in multiple folds. Connect your consultants, volunteers and agents together to have online real-time updates which can help you take immediate action as events unfold in the poll. Your situation room and war room should be tech-powered. Technology will help you make last minute pitches to voters. It will help you have direct access to those on the field protecting your interest. Ensure you are abreast of the latest tools, apps and software that will be helpful in this regard.

> *It takes an eagle-eyed and loyal agent to stand firm and stop any "robbery" that may have been planned to take place.*

Ensure People go to the Polls

It is easy for you and your supporters to become complacent on Election Day. You may have created lots of momentum and applause prior to the poll, but without all these translating to voters' turnout, your efforts will only yield zero results. On Election Day, lead the way in calling your volunteers and supporters to encourage their neighbours and everyone to go to the polls.

Call on volunteers and supporters to knock on doors for the final time to impress on people the importance of voting for you. In case the number of voters to be reached on Election Day is huge, ensure your volunteers and supporters leverage on technology to reach voters.

Your Victory and Concession Speeches

In an election, you either lose or win. There is no prize for a second place finish in most elections. Therefore, know that when the votes have been counted, you are either listed as the winner or loser. With that in mind, it is better to have two versions of your speech.

> *Technology will help you make last minute pitches to voters. It will help you have direct access to those on the field protecting your interest.*

One is the victory speech to accept your victory, outline and reiterate your goals and missions when sworn in. The other is the concession speech to show your sportsmanship, concede defeat and thank your supporters. If the speeches are not written in advance before results are finally announced, you may find yourself hurriedly scribbling something that may not totally represent what your campaign stands for.

Leave the Rest to God

Election Day is not the time to be apprehensive. You have done your part, leave the rest to God who understands the times and

136

seasons and rules in the affairs of men. Just ensure that you have actually played your own part by strategizing, campaigning, and speaking to the voters directly. When you cast your burden to God, things will be easy. You will live in perpetual peace in the midst of the storm.

WHAT TO DO POST-ELECTION (IF YOU LOSE)

What should you do when the results have been announced and they are unfavourable?

You're A Winner No Matter What

Remember the word of God that says: For whatsoever is born of God overcomes the world? As a new-breed politician, you're not fighting for victory; you were already victorious long before you even thought of contesting for any political position. Don't allow the world to determine what winning is for you. You're victorious just by stepping out to obey the call. You're victorious just by opening your mouth to proclaim the good tidings coming to your people.

> *When you cast your burden to God, things will be easy. You will live in perpetual peace in the midst of the storm.*

No one – not even election results – should define who you are. You are a winner any day, anytime. Ensure you sink that into your mind no matter the outcome of the election. Take unfavourable results in your stride. Never allow them to weigh you down. Never allow them to weigh down your resolve to see Africa become a world power. Never allow unfavourable results to make you abandon your resolve to see the African nation become a creating rather than a consuming continent.

Congratulate the winner

After it is revealed that you lost the election, in the spirit of sportsmanship please, congratulate the winner. And if you discover that there were any anomalies during the election which favoured your opponent(s), call for calm and lodge your complaints with the appropriate authorities. Call your legal advisers and strategists to plot the way forward. Never pursue frivolous lawsuits for the sake of it. Don't waste the precious time of the court. Your ambition is not worth slowing down the country's governance for.

> The other is the concession speech to show your sportsmanship, concede defeat and thank your supporters.

Take Stock

After losing an election, it is time to retreat and take stock of what you have done. Take note of what worked and what didn't work. Get the reports of your supporters, volunteers and consultants. Compare notes with independent observers to have a clearer picture of what you are dealing with.

Give Constructive Criticism

When you are in the opposition, you're expected to put the government of the day on its toes. As a genuine change agent, you will have to give constructive criticism and not just talk for the sake of it. During your time in the opposition, what will set you apart is your level of dedication to the values you have espoused on the campaign trail. That you lost the election should not make you discard them.

> During your time in the opposition, what will set you apart is your level of dedication to the values you have espoused on the campaign trail. That you lost the election should not make you discard them.

Time in opposition presents you an opportunity to put to practice some of the things you promised to do when elected. To do this successfully, your creative juices must flow optimally.

Remain Visible in a Strategic Way

Remaining front-of-the-mind among voters is a must for you, if you desire a rebound during the next election. Since it is untasteful and in some cases illegal to start another round of campaigning when the winner is just starting to govern, it is imperative to devise a method to remain in the consciousness of voters. Your creative juices need to flow in large quantity to remain in the news without coming across as overly self-promotional. Most politicians miss it at this point as they constitute themselves into a nuisance by constantly and destructively criticising the government of the day without any substance.

If you must criticise, do it constructively. Give sound advice. Don't just criticise to earn a place on the front pages of newspapers. Instead, give top-notch ideas and suggestions that cut you out as knowledgeable in governance issues.

WHAT TO DO POST-ELECTION (IF YOU WIN)

The sound of victory is sweet to the ear. It is a wonderful experience that all politicians look forward to. It is a befitting gift after days, months and even years of hard work, planning and praying. As a politician in this new era, you're born to win. So, what do you do when victory comes knocking on your door?

Thank the Voters

Thank the voters that come out to vote for you. Go on a Thank You Tour, send letters, call, email, and post on social media. Also consider sending text messages, reiterate your promises and outline the ways by which you will fulfil your promises.

> Though politicians have been associated with lies and an inability to keep promises made, the new politicians in this new era have a mandate to speak the truth and defend the truth.

Prepare for Governance

Once victory is confirmed, prepare to govern. Prepare to provide quality leadership that will be in sync with all your campaign promises. Quickly leave the celebration mood and switch to work mode. The race for Africa's greatness is not in speeches, it lies in concerted efforts and smart work.

Constitute Your Cabinet

Don't waste time. Start constituting your cabinet ASAP. Never put a square peg in a round hole. Make your cabinet a combination of the best people around that will drive your vision. The extent to which you will gain acceleration and make appreciable achievements in governance will

The fact that you have won the political battle doesn't mean the enemy will vamoose. The enemy would switch to tactical retreat and re-strategize on how to bring your government to disrepute.

depend on the kind of people that are in your cabinet. Never be ashamed to "poach" talent from those who don't belong to your political party. In fact, the criteria for choosing people in your cabinet should never be political affiliation but competence and character.

Hold Yourself Accountable to all Promises Made during Campaign

Have your promises before you every step of the way. Never allow any day pass without reminding yourself of the promises you made on the campaign trail. Though politicians have been associated with lies and an inability to keep promises made, the new politicians in this new era have a mandate to speak the truth

141

and defend the truth. Speaking the truth demands that all the promises you have made are properly documented and the plans to achieve them are also highlighted with commensurate action steps. Remember that your integrity is at stake.

> *So, never let down your guard. Never let down your spirituality.*

You must bring to pass all that you promised else you won't be different from the politicians of old who have drained Africa.

Hit the Ground Running
There is no excuse not to hit the ground running immediately you are sworn in to govern; because the vision for a new continent must be part of you before signifying interest in this position. Speed and action must be the watchword for you. Time is running out. You can't afford to dillydally. Your team must respond to any challenge that arises at the speed of light. Please note that hitting the ground running does not eliminate the need to plan and think through policies and actions. Think fast. Act fast.

Never Let Down your Guard
The fact that you have won the political battle doesn't mean the enemy will vamoose. The enemy would switch to tactical retreat and re-strategize on how to bring your government to disrepute. Know that enemies will always lurk around. Plan to deal with that reality. So, never let down your guard. Never let down your spirituality. Keep praying. Keep being holy. Keep learning. Keep strategizing.

THINK!

•It takes an eagle-eyed and loyal agent to stand firm and stop any "robbery" that may have been planned to take place.

•Technology will help you make last minute pitches to voters. It will help you have direct access to those on the field protecting your interest.

•On Election Day, lead the way in calling your volunteers and supporters to encourage their neighbours and everyone to go to the polls.

•When you cast your burden to God, things will be easy. You will live in perpetual peace in the midst of the storm.

THINK!

•During your time in the opposition, what will
set you apart is your level of dedication to
the values you have espoused on the campaign trail.
That you lost the election should not make
you discard them.

•Though politicians have been associated with lies
and an inability to keep promises made, the new
politicians in this new era have a mandate to
speak the truth and defend the truth.

•The fact that you have won the political battle
doesn't mean the enemy will vamoose. The enemy
would switch to tactical retreat and re-strategize
on how to bring your government to disrepute.

•Never let down your guard.
Never let down your spirituality.

SIGNOFF

NEVER LIVE ONLY FOR THE HISTORY BOOKS

Y ou may be the leader of the greatest nation on earth. The history books may be replete with your wondrous works here on earth. Your name may be on every lip and every media outlet may proclaim you man/woman of the century. The history of new politics and good governance in Africa may be incomplete without a chapter about you. Understand that one day, those history books will be burnt, destroyed and forgotten; but your soul will live forever.

Remember that one day, nothing else will matter except that which you do with your soul. What shall it profit you to gain the whole world and lose your own soul? Where will you be when the cloud shall break open with a loud sound from the trumpet of the archangel? Where will your soul go when it passes beyond the grave? Will your name be written in the Book of Life? Will you be welcome by the Father into eternal rest? Run for your soul. Have eternity in view. Accept Jesus as your personal lord and saviour.

Then, you can be assured of having your name in both the history books and the Book of Life!

Bibliography

Adeniji, K. (2012). *Righteous Man In Power*. Lagos: Media DNA.

Awolowo, O. (1960). *Awo*. Ibadan: The Cambridge University Press.

Azikwe, N. (1972). *My Oddyssey*. Cambridge: Cambridge University Press.

Clinton, B. (2004). *My Life*. New York: Random House.

Gergen, D. (2000). *Eyewitness To Power: The Essence of Leadership Nixon to Clinton*. New York: Simon & Schuster.

Graham, B. (1999). *Just As I Am*. San Francisco: Harper One.

Hertzberg, H. (2008, November 17). *Obama Wins*. Retrieved from The New Yorker :
http://www.newyorker.com/magazine/2008/11/17/obama-wins

House, W. (2011, February 3). *Speeches & Remarks*. Retrieved from Obama White House:
https://obamawhitehouse.archives.gov/the-press-office/2011/02/03/remarks-president-national-prayer-breakfast

King , M. L. (1958). *Stride toward freedom : the Montgomery story.* New York: Harper.

Obama, B. (2006). *The Audacity of Hope.* New York: Three River Press.

Transcript: Illinois Senate Candidate Barack Obama . (2004, July 27). Retrieved from Washington Post Website: http://www.washingtonpost.com/wpdyn/articles/A197 51-2004Jul27.html

Note

[1] Inspired from Joel 2:1-11. NKJV

[2] Inspired from Job 28:7.

[3] *I better pass my neighbor* is an expression or a relatively expensive object(s) to show off at the lower social strata in Nigeria.

[4] Proverbs 13:20 King James 2000 Bible

[5] Read more about the biography and works of Robert Greenleaf here: https://www.greenleaf.org/about-us/robert-k-greenleaf-biography/

[6] Psalm 91:1 KJV

[7] Act 17:11

[8] Joel 2:8b KJV

[9] Zechariah 2:8b KJV

[10] Inspired from Job 28:7

JOIN THE LEAGUE OF NEW BREED POLITICIANS

D o you desire integrity and excellence in Africa's politics and public service? Then join the League of New Breed Politicians.

The League of New breed Politicians (LNP) is a coalition of sincere and capable young people who have a calling in politics and desire to instill integrity and excellence in the political scene of Africa. Members of LNP subscribe to utmost integrity and excellence in public service.

LNP's core mandate is to inspire and equip sincere and capable young people to run for political office. LNP serves as a think tank to government at all levels, individuals, and corporate organizations interested in contributing to public service.

Members are drawn from all political parties, political associations, political affiliations and political organizations.

Register here: bit.ly/newpoliticians

Also from Media DNA
Righteous Man in Power

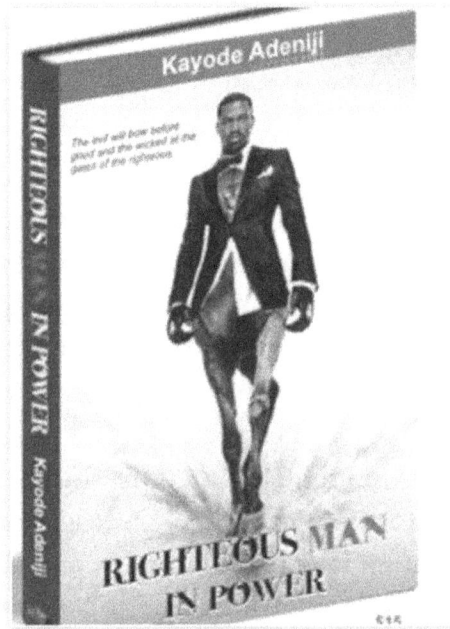

Righteous Man In Power presents the winning formula for all good and sincere people around the world, who crave for a chance to govern the affairs of men in dangerous political terrains.

Available on Amazon, Kindle and other leading bookstores worldwide. You can also order by calling +2348093061333

Hello! My Name Is Money

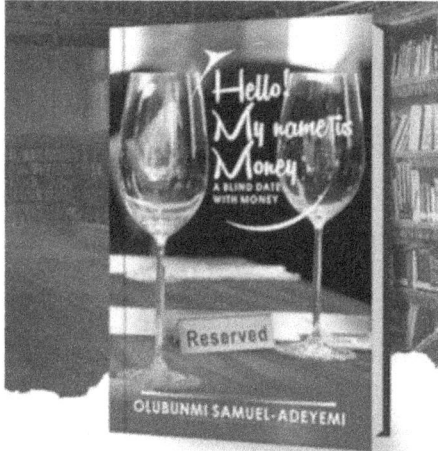

Ever imagined what a conversation with Money will look like? In this groundbreaking book, Money shares for the first time who/what it is, how to engage appropriately with it and even invites you to a limitless Source for acquiring it.

Available on Amazon, Kindle and other leading bookstores worldwide. You can also order by calling +2348093061333. Or email: books@mediadna.com.ng

Acknowledgement

I subscribe to the African proverb that it takes a community to raise a child. This resonates so well with me because at every point in my life, God has brought people my way to tutor me and shape my thinking. These people have sharpened my pen, expanded my thoughts and helped me to see possibilities.

So, first, I thank the King of Kings and Ruler of the Universe for the gift of life, favour and for the divine inspiration to write this book.

I appreciate my precious wife, Olubunmi. You're a rare gem and special gift from God to me and our children. Thank you for the painstaking reviews of the different drafts of this book. Thank you for your constant support, love and prayers. I really do love you.

My eternal gratitude goes to my parents, Mr. & Mrs. Julius Adeyemi, for the legacy of righteousness and probity bestowed on me and my siblings. We really appreciate your investments in our lives. May God keep you alive to eat the fruits of your labor. Mr. Dele Adeyemi, Mrs. Janet Anthony and Mr. Ebenezer Adeyemi, my dear siblings, I thank you for your support through the years.

I appreciate my worthy mentor, Bar. Kayode Adeniji and his wife. My wife and I deeply appreciate you for your constant guidance and selfless love. We have benefitted immensely from your message of righteousness in governance.

The ministry of Bishop David Oyedepo has greatly impacted my life and shaped my destiny. My life has not remained the same as a result of sitting under your ministration at different points in time. May God continue to increase your influence and anointing, Sir.

I bless the day God brought Rev. (Dr.) Sam and Pastor Nike Adeyemi into my life. Through your ministry, you have been prophet, pastor and teacher in the different seasons of my life. Thank you for the daily spiritual meals. My heart and leadership capacity have been expanded by learning at your feet. I found direction and purpose for my life through my contact with the ministry of Daystar Christian Center. My appreciation also goes to all the former and present associates of the ministry for the lessons learnt through everyone of you.

My parents-in-law, Engr. and Mrs. Oluwaseun Fawunmi, have displayed unrestricted kindness and love towards me from the first day we were introduced. Thank you. I recognize and appreciate this.

Dr. & Mrs. Abraham Olusola-Niyi continue to demonstrate their commitment to the advancement of my family, and we are immensely grateful.

My heartfelt appreciation also goes to the following people for their contribution to the success of this book: Mr. Segun Ogunnaike, Mr. Opeyemi Agbaje, Mr. Ekundayo Ayeni, Mr. Alexander Lawal, Mr. Babatunde Oladele, Mr. Blessing Ogunli, Mr. Olushola Adigun, and Mr. Benneth Njoku.

The following are the people who took time to read through, critic and write the Advance Praise for this book. Thank you Prof. Babs Onabanjo, Mr. Charles O'tudor, Mr. Chude Jideonwo, Mr. Johnson Abally, Dr. Kriz David, Mr. Oluseun Onigbinde, Mr. Philip Amiola and Mr. Ayobami Ilori.

I can't mention all in the 'community' deserving of my appreciation. Thank you all for touching my life positively.

www.ingramcontent.com/pod-product-compliance
Lightning Source LLC
Chambersburg PA
CBHW031208270326
41931CB00006B/463